An Analysis of

Augustine of Hippo's

The City of God
Against the Pagans

Jonathan D. Teubner

Published by Macat International Ltd
24:13 Coda Centre, 189 Munster Road, London SW6 6AW.

Distributed exclusively by Routledge
2 Park Square, Milton Park, Abingdon, Oxon OX14 4RN
711 Third Avenue, New York, NY 10017, USA

Routledge is an imprint of the Taylor & Francis Group, an informa business

www.macat.com
info@macat.com

Cataloguing in Publication Data
A catalogue record for this book is available from the British Library.
Library of Congress Cataloguing-in-Publication Data is available upon request.
Cover illustration: Ross Becker

ISBN 978-1-912453-82-5 (hardback)
ISBN 978-1-912453-64-1 (paperback)
ISBN 978-1-912453-70-2 (e-book)

Notice
The information in this book is designed to orientate readers of the work under analysis,
to elucidate and contextualise its key ideas and themes, and to aid in the development
of critical thinking skills. It is not meant to be used, nor should it be used, as a
substitute for original thinking or in place of original writing or research. References and
notes are provided for informational purposes and their presence does not constitute
endorsement of the information or opinions therein. This book is presented solely for
educational purposes. It is sold on the understanding that the publisher is not engaged
to provide any scholarly advice. The publisher has made every effort to ensure that
this book is accurate and up-to-date, but makes no warranties or representations with
regard to the completeness or reliability of the information it contains. The information
and the opinions provided herein are not guaranteed or warranted to produce particular
results and may not be suitable for students of every ability. The publisher shall not be
liable for any loss, damage or disruption arising from any errors or omissions, or from
the use of this book, including, but not limited to, special, incidental, consequential or
other damages caused, or alleged to have been caused, directly or indirectly, by the
information contained within.

CONTENTS

THE MACAT LIBRARY

The Macat Library is a series of unique academic explorations of seminal works in the humanities and social sciences – books and papers that have had a significant and widely recognised impact on their disciplines. It has been created to serve as much more than just a summary of what lies between the covers of a great book. It illuminates and explores the influences on, ideas of, and impact of that book. Our goal is to offer a learning resource that encourages critical thinking and fosters a better, deeper understanding of important ideas.

Each publication is divided into three Sections: Influences, Ideas, and Impact. Each Section has four Modules. These explore every important facet of the work, and the responses to it.

This Section-Module structure makes a Macat Library book easy to use, but it has another important feature. Because each Macat book is written to the same format, it is possible (and encouraged!) to cross-reference multiple Macat books along the same lines of inquiry or research. This allows the reader to open up interesting interdisciplinary pathways.

To further aid your reading, lists of glossary terms and people mentioned are included at the end of this book (these are indicated by an asterisk [*] throughout) – as well as a list of works cited.

Macat has worked with the University of Cambridge to identify the elements of critical thinking and understand the ways in which six different skills combine to enable effective thinking.
Three allow us to fully understand a problem; three more give us the tools to solve it. Together, these six skills make up the **PACIER** model of critical thinking. They are:

ANALYSIS – understanding how an argument is built
EVALUATION – exploring the strengths and weaknesses of an argument
INTERPRETATION – understanding issues of meaning

CREATIVE THINKING – coming up with new ideas and fresh connections
PROBLEM-SOLVING – producing strong solutions
REASONING – creating strong arguments

To find out more, visit **WWW.MACAT.COM.**

CRITICAL THINKING AND *THE CITY OF GOD*

Primary critical thinking skill: INTERPRETATION
Secondary critical thinking skill: CREATIVE THINKING

A central theme in Augustine's *City of God* is the tension between human and divine ways of organizing society. Augustine's main point is to highlight how the "city of man"—human political regimes—and the "city of God" reflect two radically different worldviews. A Christian must discover ways of existing in the "city of man" while preparing to live in the "city of God." The book as a whole attempts to offer its reader a vision for this kind of Christian existence, caught between human and divine orders.

Augustine was an intellectual and political leader of the Roman Catholic Church in the early fifth century CE. He was thus acutely aware of the challenges that Christians encountered in attempting to be both good Roman citizens and authentic Christians. As such, Augustine's *City of God* can be seen as an elaborate exercise in the critical thinking skill of interpretation. He seeks to clarify the meaning of important events (such as the Sack of Rome in 410), highlighting the problems with interpretations of that cataclysmic event, which forever changed the shape of the Western Roman Empire.

Alongside interpretation, Augustine practices creative thinking, by connecting material from the Bible and Christian history to current political and social events in a new way. By crafting and elaborating on the metaphor of "pilgrimage" to understanding the relationship between religious and non-religious ways of belonging to a political community, Augustine redefined how Western Christianity understood the relationship between religion and politics.

ABOUT THE AUTHOR OF THE ORIGINAL WORK

Augustine of Hippo was born in Thagaste (present-day Souk Ahras, Algeria) – then part of the Roman Empire – in 354 CE. He grew up in a Christian household, but initially rejected his mother's Catholic Christian faith, pursuing instead secular education and positions in the Imperial government in Italy. At 32, Augustine converted to Catholicism and in 392/3 was ordained a priest. A few years later, he was consecrated as Bishop of Hippo Regius (present-day Annaba, Algeria), a position he held for nearly 35 years. Augustine is most famous for his theological and philosophical works, including the Confessions, a narrative re-telling of his conversion to Christianity, *On the Trinity, On Christian Teaching*, and *The City of God*. Throughout his long career, Augustine was also engaged in several theological controversies on the authority of the church, the origin of human sin, and the freedom of the Christian, themes which can be traced throughout his works.

ABOUT THE AUTHOR OF THE ANALYSIS

Dr Jonathan D. Teubner is Lecturer in Religious Studies and Associate Director of the Initiative on Religion, Politics and Conflict at the University of Virginia. He received his PhD from Cambridge and was the Fernand Braudel Postdoctoral Fellow at the Laboratoire d'excellence - Religions et Sociétés dans le Monde Méditerranéen in Paris. Dr Teubner has published widely on the thought of Augustine of Hippo, including *Prayer after Augustine: A Study in the Development of the Latin Tradition* (Oxford University Press) in 2018.

ABOUT MACAT

GREAT WORKS FOR CRITICAL THINKING

Macat is focused on making the ideas of the world's great thinkers accessible and comprehensible to everybody, everywhere, in ways that promote the development of enhanced critical thinking skills.

It works with leading academics from the world's top universities to produce new analyses that focus on the ideas and the impact of the most influential works ever written across a wide variety of academic disciplines. Each of the works that sit at the heart of its growing library is an enduring example of great thinking. But by setting them in context – and looking at the influences that shaped their authors, as well as the responses they provoked – Macat encourages readers to look at these classics and game-changers with fresh eyes. Readers learn to think, engage and challenge their ideas, rather than simply accepting them.

'Macat offers an amazing first-of-its-kind tool for interdisciplinary learning and research. Its focus on works that transformed their disciplines and its rigorous approach, drawing on the world's leading experts and educational institutions, opens up a world-class education to anyone.'

Andreas Schleicher
Director for Education and Skills, Organisation for Economic
Co-operation and Development

'Macat is taking on some of the major challenges in university education ... They have drawn together a strong team of active academics who are producing teaching materials that are novel in the breadth of their approach.'

Prof Lord Broers,
former Vice-Chancellor of the University of Cambridge

'The Macat vision is exceptionally exciting. It focuses upon new modes of learning which analyse and explain seminal texts which have profoundly influenced world thinking and so social and economic development. It promotes the kind of critical thinking which is essential for any society and economy. This is the learning of the future.'

Rt Hon Charles Clarke, former UK Secretary of State for Education

'The Macat analyses provide immediate access to the critical conversation surrounding the books that have shaped their respective discipline, which will make them an invaluable resource to all of those, students and teachers, working in the field.'

Professor William Tronzo, University of California at San Diego

WAYS IN TO THE TEXT

KEY POINTS

- Augustine of Hippo was an influential Catholic theologian and bishop who is most noted for his many learned treatises and commentaries on Scripture.*

- *The City of God* argues that the two cities—the "City of Man" and the "City of God"—are mingled and intertwined in this life, but will be separated by their different loves.

- *The City of God* provides a seminal and sophisticated statement on the relationship between religion and politics in the history of Western society.

Who Was Augustine of Hippo?

Augustine of Hippo was born on November 13th 354 CE in Thagaste,* a city in the Roman province of Africa (present-day Souk Ahras, Algeria). Augustine is most widely remembered for his dense and challenging theological writings. Serving as Bishop* of Hippo Regius* (present-day Annaba, Algeria) for nearly 35 years, Augustine earned a reputation as a learned man, persuasive orator, and capable administrator. Prior to becoming bishop, Augustine had an early career as an imperial orator.

Early in life Augustine demonstrated intellectual abilities, attracting the attention of wealthy benefactors who supported his education in the Roman North African capital of Carthage. After being educated in rhetoric,* Augustine taught the subject to students in Rome and, aged 30, won a prestigious position as the imperial court orator in Milan. While in Milan, Augustine experienced a crisis of faith and started to attend the sermons of Ambrose of Milan* at the local cathedral. Augustine credits Ambrose with showing him the intellectual respectability of the Christian faith.

In August 386, Augustine converted to Christianity, a story he later told in his *Confessions*. Augustine writes of feeling suddenly overwhelmed by grief for his life of sin and in acute need of redemption.* Augustine's conversion began his five-year journey to the priesthood and later a bishopric. Between his conversion and ordination, Augustine and a core group of friends moved back to North Africa to start a proto-monastic community.* Augustine and his friends would all ascend to high positions in the Catholic Church* of Roman North Africa, dominating its politics and theology through the early decades of the fifth century. *The City of God* was written toward the end of Augustine's career as bishop and reflects his many years of teaching and learning in the Christian communities of Roman North Africa.

What Does *The City of God* Say?

The City of God was written over a fourteen-year period, between 412 and 426 CE. It is widely acknowledged as a work of scholarly and literary brilliance and continues to hold a privileged place in the history of Christian thought and Western culture more broadly. At its core is an argument over the relationship between the two cities, the "City of Man" and the "City of God." Entangled and mingled with one another, the two cities and their two loves—the "love of self" and the "love of God"—have shaped the politics and society of this world. Augustine believed that the Christian Church was on a pilgrimage* from the "earthly city" to the "heavenly city." The Church is not at home in the "earthly city," but neither is it truly an alien there: it is a temporary resident that in this life ought to work for the good of the "earthly city."

Augustine pursues this complex argument over the course of twenty-two books (or chapters). As he would later explain, he initially resolved to write *The City of God* in response to those who blamed the Christian religion for the devastation caused by the Sack of Rome* in 410. Over the course of the fourteen years it took to complete the book, Augustine turned to offering his own vision of Christian existence, inextricably caught between the "City of Man" and the "City of God." The shifting aim of the work is reflected in its two-part structure: books 1-10 attack pagan* religion, and books 11-22 turn to more substantive issues within Christian thought and practice. The first part is further divided into two parts: books 1-5 are a critique of the claim that the pagan gods provide happiness to the devout in this life, while books 6-10 are a critique of the claim that the pagan gods provide happiness in the life to come. Likewise, the second part is further divided, but into three parts: books 11-14 address the origins of the two cities, books 15-18 their history, and books 19-22 the respective ends of the two cities.

The City of God's argument has proven influential in how the Western Christian Church conceives of its relation to secular political authority. Evidence of its early reception is scant, but by the fourteenth century several learned commentaries on the full text appeared. Today *The City of God* is widely read and discussed in the fields of history, politics, and theology. Christian theologians have advocated for its importance as a foundational text (e.g., Charles Mathewes,* Robert Dodaro,* and James Wetzel*). Historians of Western political thought have increasingly recognized not only its significance in shaping the intellectual debates surrounding the relation between "Church and State,"* but also its relevance for contemporary debates on the relationship between religion and politics in pluralistic societies (e.g., John Rist,* Alasdair MacIntyre,* and Raymond Geuss*).

Why Does *The City of God* Matter?

The historical debate at the heart of the *City of God* might seem arcane and largely irrelevant to the concerns of modern life. Not only is the Roman Empire* long dead, but religion is no longer as important to our daily life as it once was. Both of these assumptions are subtly wrong in important respects. In the first case, it is true that the Roman Empire no longer exists, but that is not to say that no empires exist. The imperial form of global domination is, one might argue, not less prevalent today than it was in the first millennium of the Common Era,* although empires may now be more economic than political. The transnational ties that empires create still shape our day-to-day existence. In the second case, while religion has declined in Western Europe, it remains a significant factor in most other regions of the world, from Southeast Asia to North America. The combined forces of religious difference and imperial transnationalism* have provided a potent mixture of religious rivalry over political goods and aspirations. The twenty-first century is, in other words, just as much or more an age of empire and religious contestation as Augustine's fifth century.

Readers of *The City of God* encounter one of the first large-scale attempts to work out the dynamics of religious rivalry and transnationalism. Through this framework, Augustine recasts foundational concepts in the field of theology: the nature of blessedness, peace, and justice, and the theological virtues of faith, hope, and love. Augustine's recasting of these theological concepts in terms that political theorists and historians of Western culture would recognize has made *The City of God* one of the most important books in Western literature. As a result, *The City of God* informs many strands of theological reflection that continue to shape the political, social, and educational institutions of Western Europe (and, through lingering colonial ties, North and South America). Readers will not only encounter Augustine's fifth century Roman North

African world, but will also learn more about the fundamental tensions that lie at the heart of Western society, providing them with the tools to diagnose and analyze the increasingly intertwined worlds of religion and politics.

SECTION 1
INFLUENCES

THE AUTHOR AND THE HISTORICAL CONTEXT

KEY POINTS

- *The City of God* conveys Augustine's mature vision of Christian existence in the world.

- With his education in classical rhetoric and literature, and experience guiding the church through a tumultuous period, Augustine was uniquely able to write *The City of God*.

- The social and political strife of the years after the Sack of Rome in 410 CE is the indispensable context for understanding *The City of God*.

Why Read This Text?

Augustine of Hippo's *The City of God Against the Pagans*, usually known simply as *The City of God*, is a work of scholarly and literary brilliance unparalleled in his generation of Christian philosophers and theologians, and holds an incontestable place in the history of Christian thought and Western culture more broadly. The work exhibits familiarity with elite pagan literary culture as well as knowledge of doctrinal and social concerns within Latin Christianity* in the early century. Few people in the early fifth century had knowledge of and fluency with both of these literary traditions. A generation prior to Augustine in the Latin West,* no Christian was disposed to engage with pagan literary culture; a generation after him, there were no Christian converts who could address both Christian and pagan cultures so fluently. Although rarely read cover to cover, *The City of God* conveys Augustine's mature vision of Christian existence within the world as he and his contemporaries would have

> ❝ In this world, the two cities are indeed entangled and mingled with one another; and they will remain so until the last judgment shall separate them. ❞
>
> Augustine, *The City of God*

experienced it in the early decades of the fifth century CE. The title itself suggests its social and political importance as both a defense of Christianity's superiority over paganism ("against the pagans"), and as an account of the two cities, the "City of God" and the "City of Man."[1] For Augustine, these suggest two complementary ways of reading *The City of God*.

Author's Life

By the time he began *The City of God* in 412, Augustine was a well-known author and Bishop of Hippo Regius, a prominent port city in Roman North African (present-day Annaba, Algeria).[2] Although he was not born into the Roman nobility, Augustine was well-educated and eventually became an important bishop within the North African Catholic Church. Augustine's father was a prosperous man, but had to rely on the beneficence of much wealthier African Romans for Augustine's education, which took Augustine from his hometown of Thagaste to Carthage, Rome, and Milan. Neither Augustine's father nor his mother Monica were educated in the liberal arts,* which were available only to the elites of the Roman Empire, but their son would become one of the conduits of the liberal arts for the succeeding centuries in Latin-speaking Europe (the "West"). Despite his roaming education, Augustine ultimately made his literary reputation in North Africa. From his native shores, Augustine wrote his "great and difficult work" (*magnum opus et arduum*). It was great because of its length, and difficult because of the 14 years it took to write.[3] Because of his diverse education, experience with a range of social classes and professions, and thorough knowledge of pagan and Christian literatures, only Augustine could have written *The City of God*.

Author's Background

The context of *The City of God* is indispensable for any twenty-first-century reader to understand the work. Living in the Roman Empire as a Christian in the early decades of the fifth century was anything but a straightforward matter. In 399 ce, a pagan mob killed 60 Christians. To make matters worse, the local Senate insisted that the Church pay for the damages.[4] However Christian the Roman Empire is purported to have been in the early decades of the fifth century, Christianity had to share ideological, political, social, and religious space with paganism and other competing cultic and religious groups. This was not always easy. *The City of God* can be read as a reflection on the challenges of religious diversity.

The inter-group violence of 399 was largely both contained and containable. But things changed on August 24th, 410, when the Gothic King Alaric* led his army into the city of Rome, where they raped and pillaged for three days. It is this event that gave Augustine the final impetus to write *The City of God*. While Gothic tribes*— groups of people originating in present-day Germany and France— had been living in the Roman Empire for centuries, Romans never expected them to sack the "eternal city," as Rome was sometimes called. This event caused great alarm and uncertainty, leading to the accusation that Christianity's infidelity to Rome's pagan and secular traditions was to blame. While there is a modicum of truth to this—a wealthy Christian likely struck a deal with Alaric and opened the city gates to his army in exchange for protection[5]—Augustine took it upon himself to argue that Christians were not, in fact, to blame.

NOTES

1   Augustine, *Revisions* (New York: New City Press, 2008), 2.43.2; Augustine, *Letters 1–99*, vol. 1 (New York: New City Press, 2001), 211–70, 1*-29*; vol. 4 (New York: New City Press, 2005), 1A*.1.

2   Gerard O'Daly, *Augustine's City of God: A Reader's Guide* (Oxford: Clarendon Press, 1999), 27–36.

3   O'Daly, *Augustine's City of God: A Reader's Guide*, 35.

4   Augustine, *Letters, ep.* 50.

5   Peter Brown, *Through the Eye of a Needle: Wealth, the Fall of Rome, and the Making of Christianity in the West, 350–550 AD* (Princeton, NJ: Princeton University Press, 2012), 303.

MODULE 2
ACADEMIC CONTEXT

KEY POINTS

- Augustine wrote *The City of God* hoping to persuade pagans of the truth of Christianity.

- *The City of God* draws on the Christian apologetic tradition,* theological reflection on Scripture, and non-Christian philosophy.

- Augustine himself was influenced by both Christian and non-Christian varieties of Platonism.*

The Work in Its Context

The disciplinary classification of Augustine's *City of God* has been highly disputed in the history of scholarship. The question depends on which of the work's two purposes a reader thinks most fundamental— is it a defense of Christianity against its cultural opponents, or a more positive articulation of the vision of two cities, the "City of God" and the "City of Man," aimed at Christianity's faithful? While many of Augustine's polemics are directed against Christianity's cultured despisers, the readership of *The City of God* is not restricted to this small but interested group. Augustine dedicated the first three books to Marcellinus,* a devout Christian with whom Augustine corresponded in the years immediately before writing *The City of God*. In a letter written after the completion of *The City of God*, Augustine wrote, "For their effect is not to delight the reader or make the ignorant learn lots of things, but to persuade [the reader] that he should enter the city of God without hesitation or persevere in living there."[1] The audience of Augustine's rebuttal of pagan views is thus not those who hold those views, but rather those who might possibly be convinced by pagan

> ❝ For their effect is not to delight the reader or make the ignorant learn lots of things, but to persuade [the reader] that he should enter the city of God without hesitation or persevere in living there. ❞
>
> Augustine, *Letter to Marcellinus*

arguments against the Church. This possibility is the reason for various excursions into the intricacies of Christian doctrine, which might otherwise seem irrelevant to a treatise on the social and political life of the Christian community.

Overview of the Field

The originality of Augustine's *City of God* lies not in its theme but in its vast scope and synthesis of so many different sources and intellectual traditions. Augustine incorporates philosophically diverse themes into a sweeping narrative of the Church's pilgrimage to the "heavenly city" without eschewing the concerns of the "earthly city." The "heavenly city" refers to the community that will exist in full peace with God in the age to come and is defined by love of God and humility; the "earthly city" refers to current political regimes defined by self-love and pride. Augustine most likely had the apologetic tradition* in mind when writing the first part of the *City of God* (books 1–10). This includes the second- and early third-century Latin theologian Tertullian's* *To the Nations* and the early fourth-century Latin theologian Lactantius's* *Divine Institutions*.[2] Both texts argued against the morals of the Roman Empire and in defense of Christianity. The inspiration for the second part of *The City of God* is, however, a little more difficult to trace. Augustine took the phrase "city of God" from the Book of Psalms in the Hebrew Bible.[3] However, the plan for books 11–22 (of which 11–14 are on the origin of the two cities, 15–18 on the history of the two cities, and 19–22 on the ends of the two cities) is more complex and not straightforwardly inspired by the Psalms. *The City of God* can thus be placed at the confluence of the Christian apologetic tradition and Augustine's own engagements with Scripture.

Academic Influences

The City of God reflects Augustine's training in Christian and secular scholarly traditions. Augustine was familiar with the main currents of non-Christian philosophy and as such *The City of God* evinces the influences of Cicero,* whom Augustine read from his early days in school;[4] Varro,* to whom Augustine refers throughout *The City of God*; and Porphyry,* who according to Augustine represents the best of pagan Platonism.*

Augustine's most significant influences, however, come from within the Catholic tradition. The theological tradition in the Latin West is important to the text, particularly its doctrines of the Trinity,* creation,* and redemption.* Another important Christian influence is Ambrose, the Bishop of Milan, who baptized Augustine in 387. By the time Augustine began writing *The City of God* Ambrose had died, but his influence can be felt in the way in which Augustine synthesizes Christianity and Platonism. But above all else the Christian Scriptures are the foundation of Augustine's "great and difficult work." Augustine captured the best of pagan elite education and put it to the service of the Catholic tradition of Christianity.

If Augustine is a member of any one intellectual school, it is the Latin theological tradition that relied upon a general form of Platonism as conveyed through the writings of Plotinus,* Porphyry, and Varro. Augustine's partner in Platonism is Ambrose of Milan,* but alongside Christian Platonism Augustine was influenced by one of Ambrose's intellectual rivals, Jerome,* one of the most learned men of the fourth century and the translator of the Bible into Latin from its Hebrew and Greek sources. Jerome had little sympathy for the philosophical speculations of either Ambrose or Augustine, but shared with Augustine a commitment to the Christian Scriptures as a fount of Christian reflection. These two general influences are joined by the Latin Christian apologists, Tertullian, Cyprian,* and Lactantius. These apologists provided Augustine not only with an anti-pagan polemic, but also with a more historical outlook on the place of the Church in the world.

NOTES

1   Augustine, *Letters 1–99*, vol. 1 (New York: New City Press, 2001), 211–70, 1*–29*, 2*.3.

2   Gerard O'Daly, *Augustine's City of God: A Reader's Guide* (Oxford: Clarendon Press, 1999), 39–40.

3   Psalms 45:5, 47:2, 86:3; see also Johannes van Oort, "De Ciuitate Dei," in *Augustin Handbuch*, ed. Volker Henning Drecoll, trans. Emmanuel Rehfeld (Tübingen: Mohr Siebeck, 2007), 347–63, 249.

4   Augustine, *Confessions*, trans. Henry Chadwick (Oxford: Oxford University Press, 1991), 3.7.

THE PROBLEM

KEY POINTS

- The core question in *The City of God* is the nature and form of Christian existence in this life.

- Augustine rejected past attempts that either rejected or sacralized earthly power.

- *The City of God* attempts to move beyond any reading that strictly opposes divine and human authority.

Core Question

There is no single question or concept that is indisputably at the heart of Augustine's *City of God*. Scholars have variously argued that Augustine attempted to construct a "Christian politics" (Oliver O'Donovan*), deconstruct pagan culture (Peter Iver Kaufman*) or reconceive the boundaries of the Church (Robert Markus*). Each of these proposed aims can be observed in parts of the work. Common to them all is a more general commitment to understanding the human person as created and redeemed by Christ and to arguing that the Christian religion provides the best context and program for achieving blessedness.* The core concept is thus an understanding of corporate Christian existence within the "earthly city."

The nature of Christian existence was an important question for Augustine and his contemporaries, in light of the destruction of Rome in 410. Earlier generations of Christians—and this includes Augustine himself in his earlier thinking—interpreted the Christianization of the Roman emperors as a divine blessing of Roman rule. But what does one make of the destruction of Rome if the Christian God was supposed to be protecting it? If the political body is not divinely

> 66 Rome was invaded and sacked by the Goths under King Alaric. The attack caused great destruction. The worshippers of the many false gods blamed the Christian religion for the disaster ... Consumed with zeal for the house of God, I resolved to write the books on *The City of God* against their blasphemies and errors. 99
>
> Augustine, *Revisions*

blessed, is it then evil? Augustine preferred a middle road between interpreting the empire as divinely blessed and as an evil from which Christians must escape. In book 19, Augustine famously argued that any "earthly city" can be used, but it is only the "heavenly city" that can be truly enjoyed. This suggests that the Church more generally ought to work for the peace of the "earthly city." The precise form of Christian existence thus becomes an important question, if for no other reason than that the Church must learn to be a Church while living in the "earthly city" and identifying its good with the good of that city.

The Participants

Augustine's vision of Christian existence is a natural development from earlier thinking regarding the relationship between the Christian Church and the Roman Empire. The arguments of Lactantius and Eusebius,* two early fourth-century Church historians who were optimistic that Rome could be a vehicle to carry the Church to the "heavenly Jerusalem," were inevitably going to face trouble if the Roman Empire turned against Christianity or if the Roman Empire was destroyed. Augustine believed, contrary to this view, that the Church perseveres in spite of the vicissitudes of earthly kingdoms.

The City of God reflects this vision in its structure: books 1–10 attack pagan culture and assert the moral and rational superiority of Christianity, while books 11–22 provide more positive accounts of Christian doctrines. This background largely shaped which themes Augustine would take up. But *The City of God* enters into this debate at a particular historical moment. What scholars call "Eusebianism" *— the idea that the providential progress of history from the Incarnation of the Word of God to the conversion of the Emperor Constantine in 312 brought together the promised peace of Christ with the peace provided by the Roman Empire—came under intense scrutiny in Augustine's *City of God*. Positioning the Roman Empire as a divinely blessed political entity was, to Augustine and others, a dangerous identification of theology with state ideology.[1] The danger they perceived was giving state edicts the status of world-transcending truth. Augustine's criticism of "Eusebianism" is best seen in book 19, where he forcefully argues that all human institutions, even religious ones, are ephemeral when compared to the eternal City of God that will only be fully realized in the age to come. The Church can work for the peace of the city, but its ultimate blessedness will not be the result of any one earthly rule. Rather, the Church's blessedness will come from the promises issued by Christ, the ruler of the "heavenly city."

The Contemporary Debate

The Christian apologetic tradition argued for the moral and rational superiority of Christianity over that of paganism or other religions. An important objective of this tradition, which stretched back to the very earliest period in Christianity, was to defend Christianity against the accusations that Christians were the cause of any calamity, however minute.[2] Within this tradition, Augustine was the first major author to provide a new statement on the relationship between church and state.[3] Whereas in earlier apologetic literature, the "earthly city" was either simply rejected or sacralized in its identification with the Church, Augustine charted a middle way by arguing that one could *use* the "earthly city" and, indeed, work for its peace, but that the only sacralizable political community is the "heavenly city," which would not be realized in this world.

Augustine's *City of God* is in debt to earlier thinkers, but his relationship to prior thinking was mainly that of critique. Augustine's argument that Christians must care for the "earthly city" is relativized by his equally strong emphasis on Christians needing to find their ultimate good in the "heavenly city." This unique position between rejecting and sacralizing earthly politics inaugurated an entire epoch of Christian political thought. Unfortunately, the subtlety of this thesis was reduced to simplistic formulations in the Medieval period, which suggested that Augustine either simply rejects earthly authority or gives rulers a divine mandate. Ironically, the history of Western political thought is largely a series of misreadings of Augustine's *City of God*.

NOTES

1   Peter Van Nuffelen, *Orosius and the Rhetoric of History* (Oxford: Oxford University Press, 2012), 191–93.

2   Mark Vessey, "The History of the Book: Augustine's City of God and post-Roman Cultural Memory," in *Augustine's City of God: A Critical Guide*, ed. James Wetzel (Cambridge: Cambridge University Press, 2012), 14–32.

3   Gerard O'Daly, *Augustine's City of God: A Reader's Guide* (Oxford: Clarendon Press, 1999), 39.

THE AUTHOR'S CONTRIBUTION

KEY POINTS

- In *The City of God*, Augustine aims to sketch a theological anthropology and corporate spirituality appropriate to the Church's pilgrim status.

- The metaphor of pilgrims and pilgrimage is central to understanding Augustine's theory of Christian existence.

- Augustine prioritizes Christian scripture as a source of learning about one's commitments and obligations in political and social life.

Author's Aims

It is generally agreed that Augustine's aims in composing *The City of God* changed over the course of the 14 years (412–26) he took to write it. The work began as a defense of Christianity against pagan accusations that Rome fell to the Gothic invaders* in 410 because of the Church's infidelity to Rome. Later, the work developed into a discussion of the existence of the Christian community within the "earthly city" as it journeys to the "heavenly city." Augustine himself recognized these two aims in later comments,[1] but did not see them as being in conflict. In a seminal article in 1987, Rowan Williams* argued that *The City of God* is not a traditional study in political theory,* as it is often read, but rather a text that sketches a theological anthropology* and a corporate spirituality.*[2]

The City of God articulates Augustine's understanding of Christian existence, a theme that inevitably influences how Christians relate to other Christians, to non-Christians, and to political and social institutions. This is an ambitious goal, laid out in an equally ambitious

> ❝ Most glorious is the City of God: whether in this passing age, where she dwells by faith as a pilgrim among the ungodly, or in the security of that eternal home which she now patiently awaits until 'righteousness shall return unto judgment', but which she will then possess perfectly, in final victory and perfect peace. ❞
>
> Augustine, *The City of God*

fashion: Augustine attempts to make his argument both by questioning pagan promises of happiness in this life and the next, and drawing out the origin, history, and ends of the two cities from Christian Scriptures and the history of the Church. As such, *The City of God* is an influential proposal on how the Church is to live in the "earthly city." Despite its polemics against pagan culture, then, *The City of God* is a positive statement of how the Christian Church ought to flourish in the "earthly city" while on its pilgrimage to the "heavenly city."

Approach

Abstract notions of theological anthropology and corporate spirituality find concrete expression in Augustine's pilgrimage motif. There are countless references in the text to the Church as pilgrim, to Christ as a pilgrim, and to the suffering and pain of earthly existence as like that of a travel-weary pilgrim. So central is this image that Augustine begins the work by describing faith as pilgrimage: "Most glorious is the City of God: whether in this passing age, where she dwells by faith as a pilgrim among the ungodly..."[3] In *The City of God*, pilgrimage is a fundamental representation of the relationship between humanity and divinity.

To understand how and why pilgrimage is so significant, one must see its relation with philosophical understandings of the "ascent of the soul,"* a theme that was commonplace in ancient philosophical schools. Central to both philosophical and religious understandings of the ascent of the soul is the belief that the soul undergoes purification through intellectual and moral practices in preparation for becoming godlike. In his famous *Confessions*, Augustine foregrounded the motif of ascent, placing the motif of pilgrimage in the background. However, in *The City of God* the motif of pilgrimage takes center stage. This is not to say that *The City of God* inaugurates Augustine's pilgrimage motif, but rather that it establishes pilgrimage as a more systematic theme, which crystallizes how Augustine thinks about Christian existence in the "earthly city."

In part 2, Augustine pivots towards more specifically Christian dimensions of the ascent of the soul, integrating them into a moral and philosophical understanding of pilgrimage. A helpful way to think about pilgrimage in this context is to imagine a taking a walk that lasts a lifetime. There will, of course, be moments of physical exhaustion, but the far more challenging aspects of the journey will be psychological and moral. The blood, sweat, and tears of this life ineluctably mark it as a journey to be endured; but how and why we keep walking despite not knowing the precise end or even the nature of the obstacles is the conundrum that Augustine's *City of God* attempts to answer.

Contribution in Context

The understanding of Christian existence as a pilgrimage within a society that is neither its natural home nor its declared enemy can be traced to earlier works. Many scholars consider Augustine's *The Catechising of the Uninstructed* (*De catechizandis rudibus*), which was written around 400, to be a kind of rough draft of *The City of God*.[4] In the years immediately before he began *The City of God*, some of Augustine's letters show traces of themes that will appear in the work. In about 411, Augustine began corresponding with Flavius Marcellinus,* a devout Christian with theological interests to whom Augustine would dedicate books 1–3.[5] Marcellinus provoked some of

Augustine's early speculations on the political value of Christian forgiveness, and the arguments that this Christian practice does not undermine punitive measures that a state must perform.

The many specific lines of argumentation in *The City of God* can be traced to previous works, and scholars have spent a lifetime doing just that. But on a more basic level, it is important to appreciate the overall trajectory of Augustine's thought, from his early philosophical writings, in which he was trying to work out the relationship between his faith and the philosophical traditions that informed him to date, to the day-in-and-day-out practice of preaching and teaching the Christian scriptures, the language of which would slowly converge with his own. Like the *Confessions*, written around 397 CE, *The City of God* demonstrates how scripture provided Augustine with a critical insight into the evolving relationship of Christianity with the Roman Empire.

NOTES

1   Augustine, *Revisions* (New York: New City Press, 2008).

2   Rowan Williams, "Politics and the Soul: A Reading of the *City of God*," *Milltown Studies* 19/20 (1987): 55–72, 58.

3   Augustine, *The City of God Against the Pagans*, ed. R. W. Dyson (Cambridge: Cambridge University Press, 1998), 3.

4   Johannes van Oort, *Jerusalem and Babylon: A Study into Augustine's City of God and the Sources of His Doctrine of the Two Cities* (Leiden: E.J. Brill, 1991).

5   Augustine, *Letters 100–155*, vol. 2 (New York: New City Press, 2002); see letters 136, 138–39.

SECTION 2
IDEAS

MODULE 5
MAIN IDEAS

KEY POINTS

- The main themes of *The City of God* are the two cities, pilgrimage, and God's providential ordering of the "earthly city."

- Blessedness, peace and justice are the goods that the Church is trying to acquire in the "heavenly city."

- Augustine clarifies relation between two cities by appeals to oppositions, such as the "love of God" and the "love of self."

Key Themes

The main themes of Augustine's *City of God* are the two cities, the pilgrimage from the earthly to the heavenly city, and God's providential structuring of the "earthly city" as the way towards the "heavenly city." While there is a tight conceptual relationship between these themes, they are not equally present in the text. The theme of the two cities dominates, and Augustine explicitly refers back to this throughout the 22 books of *The City of God*. The theme of pilgrimage, too, is consistently appealed to through the work, though less dominant. The theme of providence,* however, is more subtly developed in the text, and a reader might easily overlook this aspect. It slowly emerges in scattered comments, culminating in Augustine's major statement in book 19 of the providential ordering of the "earthly city" as a way for the Church to travel to the "heavenly city."

Books 1–10 are ostensibly dedicated to a defense of Christianity against pagan accusations that Rome was destroyed because of the infidelity of Christians towards Rome's pagan and secular* traditions;

> ❝ It will not, indeed, possess it in the end, because it does not make good use of it before the end. For the time being, however, it is advantageous to us also that this people should have such peace in this life; for, while the two cities are intermingled, we also make use of the peace of Babylon. ❞
>
> Augustine, *The City of God*

however, the first five books are effectively an argument against the happiness that pagan culture promises in this life and the next. It is not until part 2, books 11–22, that Augustine develops the themes of the two cities, pilgrimage, and providence in earnest. Augustine presents the historical development of two societies organized according to different loves—love of self in the "earthly city," and love of God in the "heavenly city." In books 11–14, Augustine accounts for the origin of the two cities, then, in books 15–18, details the course they take throughout history, and finally, in books 19–22, identifies the end towards which they are moving. While the two cities are, for Augustine, separate entities in the next age, here in this age they are intermingled. Moreover, those who are members of the "heavenly city" get there only by way of the "earthly city." God's providence is therefore seen in the fact that one arrives at the "heavenly city" by way of its navigation of the "earthly city."

Exploring the Ideas

Underlying Augustine's understanding of the providential ordering of the two cities are the concepts of blessedness, peace,* and justice:* all three have counterparts in the "earthly city," but are only perfectly realized in the "heavenly city."

Augustine's notion of blessedness is the continual and stable enjoyment of God. As he puts it at 11.13, blessedness "will result from a conjunction of two things: namely, the enjoyment without interruption of the immutable Good which is God; and the certain knowledge, free from all doubt and error, that it will remain in the same enjoyment forever."[1] His notion of peace is that of an ordered and harmonious life, as he suggests at 19.13: "The peace of all things lies in the tranquility of order; and order is the disposition of equal and unequal things in such a way as to give to each its proper place."[2]

Augustine's notion of justice is a little more complex, bridging the "earthly city" and the "heavenly city." He describes at 19.4: "there is established in man himself a certain just order of nature, such that the soul is subordinated to God and the body to the soul, and thus both body and soul are subordinated to God."[3] Acts of justice, which include, for Augustine, rightly submitting lower things to higher things (body to soul, soul to God, and so on), move a society closer to peace. Perfect justice and peace thus converge in the heavenly city.

Augustine believes that blessedness, peace, and justice are only realizable in the "heavenly city," and are only experienced in impoverished form in the "earthly city." This distinction, to many readers, restricts the usefulness of these ideas because they do not fully apply to everyday life. Blessedness, peace, and justice should, however, move people to work for justice and practice patience within the existing world, even though they will be inadequately realized here.

Language and Expression

Augustine can often stray into extended debates about the nature of happiness or the suitability of emotions, so it is helpful for the reader to keep in mind a few signposts that organize the text.

The first of these is rhetorical device of oppositions. Oppositions—between pride and humility, love of self and love of God, time and eternity, and so on—are interlaced throughout the text. These should remind the reader of the foundational opposition between the "City of God" and the "City of Man." Another signpost is the goal-oriented structure of the relationships between "science"* and "wisdom."* "Science" is, for Augustine, not restricted to the natural sciences such as biology or physics, but refers more generally to the human comprehension that is possible in this life; "wisdom" is a kind of knowledge that is principally the enjoyment of God, and is only achievable by a perfectly just and holy person in the "heavenly city." "Wisdom" is, for Augustine, "science's" goal. Another signpost is the status Augustine gives to present political circumstances. The Roman Empire is neither the unqualifiedly evil "City of Man" represented by "Babylon," nor is it the divinely blessed eternal city of "Jerusalem," but these are often appealed to as logical endpoints.

The sheer size of Augustine's work makes it challenging for the reader to develop a nuanced and critical approach to the text, the kind of approach that would normally be cultivated through slow, careful reading habits. In the light of this difficulty, it is helpful to keep in mind the person of Jesus Christ and the role he plays in both Augustine's polemical attack on pagan culture and the more positive argument regarding the origins, histories, and ends of the two cities. For Augustine, Christ is both "science" and "wisdom," and by practicing Christ's virtues one may cultivate "wisdom." Moreover, Augustine depicts Christ on a pilgrimage in his Incarnation, and our pilgrimage is achieved by embodying the virtues of Christ—humility, patience, faith, hope, and love.

NOTES

1 Augustine, *The City of God Against the Pagans*, ed. R. W. Dyson (Cambridge: Cambridge University Press, 1998), 466. See also Augustine's comments vis-à-vis Platonist conceptions of blessedness/happiness at 8.8.

2 Augustine, *The City of God Against the Pagans*, 938.

3 Augustine, *The City of God Against the Pagans*, 921.

MODULE 6
SECONDARY IDEAS

KEY POINTS

- Faith, hope, and love provide the theological foundation on which Augustine's more nuanced arguments are grounded.

- Augustine argues that communities are defined by what they love and that the two cities are created out of "love of self" and "love of God."

- The specifically theological features of Augustine's argument have been relatively overlooked.

Other Ideas

Augustine's *City of God* is an ineluctably theological text. It is no surprise, then, that the theological virtues*—faith, hope and love— are consistently interlaced throughout all 22 books. These three virtues are accompanied by three affective responses: patience, desire, and joy. While the three theological virtues have an unmistakable biblical inspiration (1 Corinthians 13:13), Augustine's coordination of faith, hope, and love with the affective responses of patience and desire—patience *with* the "earthly city" and desire *for* the "heavenly city"—is a subtle but important development in the history of theology. Prior to Augustine there was not much in-depth moral or psychological treatment of the three theological virtues. Augustine further highlights that, among these virtues, love and joy are the only ones that will continue into the "heavenly city." That is to say, faith, hope, desire, and patience will all pass away, but the virtue of love and the affection of joy will abide in the City of God.[1] By weaving the theological virtues into the concrete political conditions of an "earthly city," which one must endure and make use of, Augustine

> **❝** Two cities, then, have been created by two loves: that is, the earthly by love of self extending even to contempt of God, and the heavenly by love of God extending to contempt of self. **❞**
>
> Augustine, *City of God*

offers a new vision of how one must live in the "earthly city" while on pilgrimage to the "heavenly city."

Exploring the Ideas

Augustine's *City of God* offers an original synthesis of the theological virtues and action that influenced an entire epoch within Europe, the so-called "Middle Ages" (roughly speaking, 500–1500 CE). The role of the theological virtues can be seen in their relation to the concepts of blessedness, peace, and justice. In other words, one can detect the theological virtues of faith, hope, and love, and their affective responses patience, desire, and joy as they support and fill out the notions of blessedness, peace, and justice. The combination of Augustine's articulation of these nine ideas (faith, hope, love, patience, desire, joy, blessedness, peace, and justice), all of which are derived from the Christian scriptures, forms a complex picture of how one might live in the "earthly city" while on pilgrimage to the "heavenly city."

A helpful way to understand the role of the theological virtues is to think about how their opposites function. The opposite of, say, "love of God," is not "hate of God," but rather "love of self."[2] The theological virtue of love is defined, for Augustine, as an inclination or striving that flows from the will and becomes concrete through the object loved. There is therefore a tight relationship between the lover, the love, and the beloved. In other words, *what* one loves is central to the nature of the love itself. In *The City of God*, one of the primary oppositions is between "love of God" and "love of self." This opposition functions as a foundational dynamic in understanding how the Church can realize blessedness, peace, and justice: "Two cities, then, have been created by two loves: that is, the earthly by love of self extending even to contempt of God, and the heavenly by love of God extending to contempt of self." (14.28) Furthermore, the proper affective response to love is the opposite of contempt, which is enjoyment or joy. Augustine believes that the Church will find joy not simply in loving, but in loving *God*. This same structure could be applied to faith and hope.

Overlooked

The City of God has been the subject of innumerable theological, political, philosophical, and historical investigations. It is considered, on the one hand, as a text that presents a Christian philosophy of history, and, on the other, as a major statement of the political attitude a Western Christian should have towards temporal political and social institutions. What has been overlooked or neglected by contemporary scholarship is, surprisingly, the profoundly theological basis of its philosophical, political, and historical material.

Rowan Williams[3] and Oliver O'Donovan,[*4] among others, have sought to refocus attention on the theological basis of Augustine's *City of God*. The central reason their mode of reading the text has failed to receive significant attention is that political readings still dominate the field. These readings are, to a large extent, indebted to the work of Robert Markus,[*] whose *Saeculum: History and Society in the Theology of St Augustine* was a major contribution to the field of "political theology." It advanced a reading according to which Augustine proposed the existence within this age of a neutral space in which both Christians and non-Christians could work to the good of the "earthly city." Markus's work was originally published in 1970, and has since set the course for the dominant discourse on *The City of God*.

However, as "secularism"[*]—the notion that there is a neutral sphere of activity that is free of any particular religious commitments—

has continued to come under fire in the late decades of the twentieth century and the first decades of the twenty-first century, Markus's so-called "secularist" reading of *The City of God* has seemed less plausible. This suggests that Markus's cultural context guided his reading of the text, a point he himself acknowledged in his later *Christianity and the Secular*.[5] With the waning of secularism, Augustine's *City of God* is ripe for reconsideration.

If readers were to take up a more thoroughly theological reading of the text, the first ten books would seem more relevant to fully understanding Augustine's apologetic project in the *City of God*. Accordingly, the first ten books, being an assault on pagan religious belief in particular, should be considered an important first step in Augustine's efforts to demonstrate the value of a life based on Christian commitments and how these might be possible within a society that is largely guided by pagan or non-Christian laws and commitments. Furthermore, this reading would cohere with Augustine's use of the pilgrimage image: Augustine transformed this biblical idiom into a set of doctrines on how the Christian might navigate his political, social and cultural context in exclusively Christian terms.

NOTES

1 Augustine, *The City of God Against the Pagans*, ed. R. W. Dyson (Cambridge: Cambridge University Press, 1998), 1182.

2 Augustine, *The City of God Against the Pagans*, 609.

3 Rowan Williams, *On Augustine* (London: Bloomsbury, 2016).

4 Oliver O'Donovan, *The Problem of Self-Love in St. Augustine* (New Haven, CT: Yale University Press, 1980); "The Political Thought of *City of God* 19" in Oliver O'Donovan and Joan Lockwood O'Donovan, eds. *Bonds of Imperfection: Christian Politics, Past and Present* (Grand Rapids, MI: Eerdmans Press, 2004), 48-72.

5 Robert Markus, *Christianity and the Secular* (Notre Dame, IN: University of Notre Dame Press, 2006).

MODULE 7
ACHIEVEMENT

KEY POINTS

- Augustine's *City of God* "came of age" in the Renaissance, when it was first read with serious attention.

- Despite being widely read today, it is indisputably a text that speaks from and about concerns that existed in the early fifth century.

- The major limitations of *The City of God* have been exhibited by attempts to establish and defend an earthly Christendom.

Assessing the Argument

Augustine's *City of God* has grown in relevance over the course of its nearly 1600 years of existence, but it had a slow start. It was not until the fourteenth century that Nicholas Trevet* and Thomas Waleys,* two English members of the Dominican Order,* began to expand its reputation by writing commentaries on it.[1] *The City of God's* broader influence began to pick up pace when the Italian poet and scholar Petrarch* (1304–74) paid it an unusual compliment by including it in a list of his favorite books. Augustine's *City of God* was for the first time set alongside Cicero's *Republic* and Seneca's* *Moral Epistles*.[2] By the time of the Protestant Reformation,* Augustine's great work on the two cities was being used in criticism of the Roman Catholic Church, whose scholars had themselves begun to rely on a reading of *The City of God* that stressed the connection between the Church and the "heavenly city" Augustine praises in his text.

The City of God, then, is largely a text made important by the European Renaissance,* a period when the arts and sciences in

> ❝ Augustine is neither a philosopher of the ancient world nor a proto-medieval thinker. Nor is he a Christian whose Christianity is neatly detachable from his philosophical engagements. He is a philosophically Christian thinker whose famous but yet to be deciphered antitheses—two cities, two loves, two ends—can still challenge the parodies that we would make of them. ❞
>
> James Wetzel, *Augustine's* City of God*: A Critical Guide*

European cities flourished as they hadn't since the heyday of ancient Greece* and Rome. It was at this point that Augustine's large-scale understanding of the relationship between the two cities, his conception of divine providence, and his pilgrimage motif started to proliferate in learned circles. The Renaissance thinker and Reformation theologian John Calvin* found inspiration in *The City of God*, reading it as a critique of the Roman Catholic Church.[3] This was a common theme for Protestant Reformation theologians, who protested against abuses in the Roman Catholic Church and began to form their own Christian denominations in the sixteenth century. Martin Luther,* Father of the Reformation and himself an Augustinian monk before "protesting" against the Roman Catholic hierarchy, consistently called on Augustine's works, including *The City of God*, in his polemics against his Roman Catholic adversaries.[4]

Achievement in Context
Augustine's influence is almost unparalleled in Western and Western-influenced civilizations. The most immediate organs of his influence are the Christian churches—especially the Roman Catholic Church, which has been more explicitly devoted to the Bishop of Hippo's

teachings than other churches. Augustine's influence also extends to what Abraham Kuyper* called the "three great Calvinist countries"—the Netherlands, Great Britain, and the United States of America.[5] While *The City of God* is only rarely read cover to cover by any political figure, the ideas and themes contained in Augustine's "great and difficult work" have been influential in the formation of Western political institutions.

Despite the continued vitality of Augustine's "great and difficult work," readers should not be lulled into thinking that our social and cultural contexts are those of Augustine. Indeed, one can see the effect of changing social and cultural conditions on the vastly various interpretations of *The City of God* through its nearly 1600 years of readership. These variations are often a result of focusing on one aspect of the work. For example, readers influenced by apocalypticism*—that is, the belief that the end of the world is imminent—focused on Augustine's discussion of the day of judgment, hell, and heaven; readers who found themselves in conflict with non-Christian cultures often focused on the early books, in which Augustine launches a full assault on pagan culture; and readers who found themselves in an environment of political and religious pluralism looked to Augustine's discussion of the people of God as a pilgrim people, who are merely wayfarers in this world.

Augustine's *City of God* dates from what was a tumultuous time for the Mediterranean world. It inaugurated a focus on a set of questions—and attempts to answer those questions—that are now associated with Western European culture. This is a predictable outcome of Augustine's concerns in *The City of God*. While Augustine mentions the history of the Levant and Subcontinent, he does so only in reference to the formation of Western Christianity. Even the Greek-speaking Eastern church of Augustine's time would have struggled to find application for a text inspired by the fall of Rome, since the Roman Empire was still strong in Constantinople* and the Eastern Mediterranean lands it controlled.

Limitations

Augustine's *City of God* most commonly meets its limitations in the political applications of its enthusiastic readership. These applications have often pushed beyond Augustine's text and generated some infelicitous results. A common example is the interpretation of Augustine's text as a "charter for Christendom.*"[6] Arguments for this reading are in debt to certain medieval interpretations of passages from book 19, which out of context might be seen as suggesting that for earthly peace to be possible a Christian emperor must rule. While the ill effects of divinizing the earthly ruler must be acknowledged, Pope Gregory VII's* use of this "charter" gave him the broad vision that led to the renaissance of the liberal arts curriculum in Europe. The effects of Gregory's reforms were not fully felt until centuries later, when the training curricula of monasteries were more explicitly organized according to the vocational demands of being a priest. The newly forming universities of the twelfth to fourteenth centuries embodied this development of providing vocational training to future priests. Augustine would not have been surprised to learn that thinking about Christian existence and society would bring about new ways of living as a "pilgrim" in this world, but his agnosticism* with regard to the eternal value of political reforms would have tempered his support for Gregory VII.

NOTES

1   Johannes van Oort, *Jerusalem and Babylon: A Study into Augustine's City of God and the Sources of His Doctrine of the Two Cities* (Leiden: E.J. Brill, 1991), 5.

2   Bonnie Kent, "Reinventing Augustine's Ethics: The Afterlife of *City of God*," in *Augustine's City of God: A Critical Guide*, ed. James Wetzel (Cambridge: Cambridge University Press, 2012).

3   John Calvin, *Institutes of the Christian Religion*, rev. (Peabody, MA: Hendrickson Publishers, 2007), Book 4, Chapter 2.

4   Albrecht Beutel, "Luther," in *Augustin Handbuch*, ed. Volker Henning Drecoll (Tübingen: Mohr Siebeck, 2007), 615–22.

5   Abraham Kuyper, *Lectures on Calvinism* (Grand Rapids, MI: William B. Eerdmans, 1994), 3.

6   J. O'Meara, *Charter of Christendom: The Significance of the "City of God"* (New York: Macmillan, 1961).

MODULE 8
PLACE IN THE AUTHOR'S WORK

KEY POINTS

- *The City of God* is Augustine's most extended and erudite treatise on his pastoral ambitions for the Church.

- The entanglement of the two cities in this world is an occasion for trusting that God's providence will bring about peace and justice.

- *The City of God* is an important and influential work because it is a summary of a wide-range of Augustine's philosophical, historical, and theological opinions.

Positioning

Augustine began *The City of God* at the midpoint of his literary career, which spanned forty-two years, from 388 to his death in 430. His longest treatise, *The City of God* is the product of a mature thinker, who had honed his philosophical, historical, and theological opinions through multiple controversies, church councils, and countless other works. *The City of God* is not so much the distillation of Augustine's lifetime's work, but rather a catalogue or encyclopedia of the theological and philosophical questions that occupied Augustine throughout his life. In one part, Augustine discusses the role of free will, in another the role of human emotions, in another the intricacies of a doctrine of God, and in still another the more pointedly political issues that confront the Christian Church. What holds these concerns together is Augustine's lifelong commitment to the care of Christian souls in this world. If nothing else, Augustine was a pastor, taking his duties as Bishop of Hippo seriously. Despite its cultural polemics, philosophical debates, and arcane doctrinal disputes, *The City of God* is

> **❝** Late have I loved you, beauty so old and so new:
> late have I loved you. And see, you were within and
> I was in the external world and sought you there,
> and in my unlovely state I plunged into those lovely
> created things which you made. You were with me,
> and I was not with you. **❞**
>
> Augustine, *Confessions*

Augustine's most pastoral work and stands as his mature formulation of the Church's existence within the "earthly city." *The City of God* thus brings together many lines of thought within Augustine's overarching vision.

Integration

It is difficult to identify unifying themes in Augustine's extensive corpus, so to say how *The City of God* anticipates Augustine's later work is far from straightforward. That is not to say that Augustine's work is just "one thing after another"—scholars have long argued for one unifying theme or another, whether that is Augustine's Christology,* ecclesiology,* or anthropology. Thankfully, one does not have to settle on a single, indisputably essential doctrine of Augustine's thought. Rather, it is better to think of Augustine having an approach or an ethos: while he is certainly interested in philosophical technicalities, Augustine was too concerned with addressing the immediate demands of his community to make sure what he said perfectly cohered with what he said yesterday, last year, or in his very first book. Augustine's work can thus be characterized by a concern to address the challenges of his community and to instruct those willing to listen how they might discover their vocation in relinquishing their pride and personal control to God.

The central insight of Augustine's literary career—that in our searching for God we discover that he was always there—set the stage for his last major phase after *The City of God*—namely, his anti-Pelagian* writings. These attempted to counter Pelagius'* reduction of the role of divine grace in the salvation of mankind. Though there is some evidence in *The City of God* of the doctrine of grace* that he later developed,[1] Pelagianism* does not emerge as a major polemical target in this work. However, the ethos just described is what most rankled Pelagius and his supports: the Christian's abdication of full responsibility to improve oneself. In the terms of *The City of God*, the two irreversibly entangled cities are, for Augustine, a tragic part of the providential order, and the reason we must search for God in this world; if Pelagius had used Augustine's terms, he would have presented the disentanglement of the two cities as yet another task for humanity to solve—and failing to do so would count against us.

Significance

Augustine is one of the founts of Western literary culture, and to this day one can find his influence in Christian and secular texts alike. His corpus, from the early philosophical dialogues to his late anti-Pelagian polemics, is unparalleled in its influence on the Western intellectual tradition.

Augustine was not the only influential voice from the fifth century. Others, such as John Cassian,* would provide alternative traditions in the early Middle Ages* and beyond. However, by the mid-seventh century Augustine had become an authoritative theologian, with whom subsequent Latin theologians wanted to show their agreement and engagement. It is impossible to say that Augustine gained this status by virtue of any one work. It is more likely that Augustine's authority was a result of having written so much over the course of his life. As his longest single treatise, *The City of God* has rarely been read from cover to cover, even among theologians. Its most influential passages—those accusing pagan Rome of crimes, containing advice to "Christian rulers," or outlining his speculations on hell—would be passed down in excerpted form during the Middle Ages and Renaissance, divorced from their original literary context. Augustine is not Augustine because he wrote *The City of God*; rather, *The City of God* is *The City of God* because Augustine wrote it.

NOTES

1   Robert Dodaro, *Christ and the Just Society in the Thought of Augustine* Cambridge: Cambridge University Press, 2004).

SECTION 3
IMPACT

MODULE 9
THE FIRST RESPONSES

KEY POINTS

- Most early responses were directed at specific points Augustine made and did not address the overall narrative or argument.

- We lack evidence of any substantial or prolonged debate on *The City of God* immediately after its publication.

- The scholarly consensus holds that *The City of God* aligns with the views Augustine espoused in the anti-Pelagian controversy.

Criticism

The City of God did not make quite the literary splash one might expect, given Augustine's standing. In fact, it was not until the fourteenth century that the first commentaries on the work were written. Sadly, then, we know very little regarding readers' response to and criticism of *The City of God* within Augustine's lifetime, which includes the pagan reception of Augustine's long account of the superiority of Christianity over its cultural rival.

While we do not have records of the early responses to Augustine's text, we do know that a certain Firmus,* after having heard *The City of God*'s very long book 18 read aloud over the course of three afternoons, requested the whole of the text.[1] However, this request was, it seems, unusual (though a sure sign of enthusiasm for what he heard). The earliest confirmed criticism of *The City of God* occurs roughly 100 years after its publication, which should give us some idea how scholars would have responded to Augustine's great work within his lifetime. In the early sixth century, Boethius* offered what many scholars

> ❝ You must however examine whether the seeds of argument sown in my mind by St. Augustine's writings have borne fruit. ❞
>
> Boethius, *On the Trinity*

would now consider to be a critique of Augustine's reconciliation of human freedom and an all-knowing God (contained in book 5). Augustine believed that God, being timeless, was able to foresee what humans would choose of their own free will. However, Boethius thought that the fact that God is timeless did not genuinely clear the way for human freedom: if God's knowledge of the future is infallible, an uncontroversial entailment of God's foreknowledge, how could the future not already be determined? Related to this, Boethius in his fifth theological tractate, *Against Eutyches and Nestorius*, also appealed to Augustine's distinction between eternity as timelessness and eternity as everlasting. The first responses were most likely very similar to Boethius's—directed at specific arguments in the books or sections that were available.

Responses

As an attentive reader might expect, we do not have records of Augustine's responses to criticisms of *The City of God*. Even in his *Revisions* (*Retractiones*), Augustine did not find anything he thought best to reconsider. This makes it difficult to say anything definite about either the criticisms or Augustine's responses. Be that as it may, one can speculate that the reason Augustine did not have anything to revise is that the work was originally written with an eye to the Pelagian controversy, the major impetus for his reconsiderations.[2] That would suggest that his Pelagian opponents might have thought that *The City of God* too heavily emphasized the role of divine grace in human action (thus de-emphasizing human responsibility). This dialogue certainly took place in Augustine's so-called "anti-Pelagian writings." However, *The City of God* did not figure prominently in this critical dialogue, which dominated the final years of Augustine's life.

Augustine was, then, largely happy with this "great and difficult work." If there were substantial criticisms of Augustine's work, they are unknown today. Present-day speculations regarding the nature of the criticisms and Augustine's response are thus largely based on later readings of *The City of God*. Again, it was not until the fourteenth century that theologians (e.g., Nicholas Trevet* and Thomas Waley*) started to take an interest in the work as a whole, or, for that matter, started to read it at all.[3] Literarily and philosophically speaking, then, Augustine's *City of God* did not gain attentive readers or relevant criticism until almost 1000 years after it was written. Prior to that point, people read sections of the work, usually in excerpted forms, and largely tried to draw on the authority of Augustine to support their various causes, whether the Bishop of Hippo seemed to agree or not in the actual text of *The City of God*.

Conflict and Consensus

Augustine's post-*City of God* literary career was almost entirely consumed by the later stages of the Pelagian controversy. More than anything else, Augustine's response to his Pelagian critics (e.g., Julian of Eclanum*), who faulted him for ignoring or downplaying the role of the individual human will in loving God and living a holy life, has framed how his corpus is interpreted as a whole. This is not necessarily wrong-headed, for the theme of grace and the importance of divine assistance for securing the possibility and stability of loving God is indeed a central theme for Augustine. The consensus view of *The City of God* is that, whether or not it was explicitly intended to, it aligns with Augustine's anti-Pelagian views.

An area of more conflict than consensus is the debate regarding *The City of God*'s presentation of the relationship between religion and politics. In broader debates, *The City of God* informs a politics of Christian engagement. All those who appeal to Augustine's "great and difficult work" argue for a place for religious belief in contemporary political discourse and decision-making processes, a case that, with some setbacks, has been successfully advanced in the early decades of the twenty-first century. While virtually no scholar argues that Augustine advocated for anything close to a "theocracy"* (that is, rule according to religious teachings), most accept that a person's religious beliefs cannot be neatly separated from his or her economic, political, social, and cultural decisions.

NOTES

1   Augustine, *Letters 1–99*, vol. 1 (New York: New City Press, 2001), 211–70, 1*-29*, 1A*.1, 2*.3.

2   See Robert Dodaro, *Christ and the Just Society in the Thought of Augustine* (Cambridge: Cambridge University Press, 2004).

3   Bonnie Kent, "Reinventing Augustine's Ethics: The Afterlife of *City of God*," in *Augustine's City of God: A Critical Guide*, ed. James Wetzel (Cambridge: Cambridge University Press, 2012).

MODULE 10
THE EVOLVING DEBATE

KEY POINTS

- Augustine's *City of God* is most influential in the sub-field of political theology.*

- Three schools of thought—"liberal," "conservative," and "radical"—have emerged from recent debates on *The City of God*.

- In current scholarship, it is mainly Anglophone Protestants that are probing the meaning and application of *The City of God.*

Uses and Problems

Augustine's *The City of God* has wide influence in the arts, humanities, and social sciences, and so is too diffuse to recognize easily, especially as regards its marginal arguments. In the fourteenth century, interest in the text concentrated on its knowledge of antiquity—there was no other widely distributed source on the history, practices, and culture of ancient Rome. In the fifteenth and sixteenth centuries, the Salamancan* school focused on Augustine's theory of utility (how and when certain things should be used) in *The City of God*. In subsequent centuries, Augustine's *City of God* came to be read as a charter of Church–State relations,* and a vision of the place of scientific development within society.[1]

In the late nineteenth and twentieth centuries, when academics began to separate fields of inquiry into disciplines (such as classics, theology, philosophy, literature, physics, and chemistry), *The City of God*'s influence was mainly restricted to politics and theology. This specialization allows us to chart the text's influence on certain debates.

> ❝ A re-reading of the *City of God* will allow us to realize that political theology can take its critique, both of secular society and of the Church, directly out of the developing Biblical tradition, without recourse to any external supplementation. For within Augustine's text we discover the *original* possibility of critique that marks the western tradition. ❞
>
> John Milbank, *Theology and Social Theory: Beyond Secular Reason*

For example, the field of political theology was, more or less, created by reactions to and readings of Augustine's *City of God*. Beyond this sub-discipline of theology, Augustine's work has influenced the evolution of philosophical and theological anthropology, the philosophy of history,* and Biblical studies.*

Schools of Thought

Though *The City of God* was not often read comprehensively until the fourteenth century, it inspired several significant writers and thinkers. Notable examples include Thomas Aquinas,* John Calvin,* Ernst Troeltsch,* Hannah Arendt,* and Reinhold Niebuhr,* all attracted to ideas within Augustine's work, but also pushing beyond it for answers to their questions and concerns. From responses to *The City of God* in the twentieth century, three schools of thought emerged—"liberal," "conservative," and "radical."

The "liberal" school formed around political readings of book 19. Its prominent figures include Arendt and Niebuhr, who adopt Augustine's historical-developmental outlook on how politics and ethics are formed. Within these historically formed politics and ethics, the conditions for human flourishing are found. Niebuhr identifies the role of religious belief in shaping engagement with worldly institutions, whether the family or politics. Though inspired by

Augustine's *City of God,* both Arendt and Niebuhr stop short of endorsing Augustine's positions on religious coercion and hell.[2]

In contrast to this "liberal" tradition, a more recent, "conservative" school of thought emerged from a stronger theological reading of the text. Oliver O'Donovan* argues, partly on the basis of his reading of book 19, for the importance of the established Church in contemporary British society.[3] There are many younger scholars of this school in the United Kingdom and in the United States. This interpretation prioritizes the theological features of *The City of God*, reading it as a work on the origins and foundations of moral order.

The "radical" interpretative tradition, led by John Milbank,* contrasts itself with both these camps.[4] Scholars within this tradition come under the banner of "Radical Orthodoxy,"* a school of thought that began in Cambridge in the 1990s, whose members found common cause in their dissatisfaction with modernity. Like O'Donovan, Milbank argues for a stronger theological reading, but emphasizes the critique of society in *The City of God*. Known for his bold polemical style, Milbank adopts Augustine's spirit and attitude as much as the actual content of his text. One of Milbank's students, Graham Ward,* now Regius Professor of Divinity at the University of Oxford, has continued this line of attack with a critique of modernity entitled *Cities of God,* focusing on desire in the formation of communities.[5]

In Current Scholarship

Major proponents of *The City of God*'s core project are located in the United States and the United Kingdom: in America, the philosopher Nicholas Wolterstorff* stands out for his constructive use of Augustine's *City of God*; and in Britain, the theologians Oliver O'Donovan, Rowan Williams, and John Milbank* have each used the work to argue for a specific relation between church and state. Wolterstorff is a Reformed Protestant,* while O'Donovan, Williams, and Milbank are Anglicans.* In part because of their historical entanglement with the abuse of political authority, these Protestant denominations have long puzzled over the role of Christian existence within a democratic political and social order. Both the Reformed and Anglican traditions have been used to justify coercive regimes across the world. These tragic histories provide impetus for scholars to consider how Christians can live in an uncertain age with an ambiguous relationship to earthly institutions.

The City of God is more central to the work of O'Donovan and Milbank. O'Donovan has penned several seminal articles and books on Augustine's political theory. He is currently writing a systematic moral theology drawing on Augustine's *City of God*.[6] Although Milbank has not contributed to scholarly discussion on *The City of God*, his *Theology and Social Theory* draws on it fruitfully. Unlike Milbank, O'Donovan—a Church of England priest—has contributed to the scholarly discussion regarding the relationship between Augustine's "City of Man" and "City of God." Both are Augustinian lines of inquiry, but each attracts a different audience, depending on theological style.

Wolterstorff and Williams have a lighter, less direct relationship with *The City of God*. Both have written on specific themes within Augustine's work, but when they turn to more constructive comments Augustine fades into the background. They share Augustine's view that politics is a sphere of limited but necessary good. To work for the peace of the "earthly city" is a good, but the final good towards which all things strive rests in the "heavenly city."

NOTES

1   Ernest L. Fortin, "Augustine, the Arts, and Human Progress," in *Human Rights, Virtue, and the Common Good*, ed. J. Brian Benestad (London: Rowman and Littlefield, 1996).

2   See Hannah Arendt, *The Human Condition*, 2nd ed. (Chicago: University of Chicago Press, 1998) and *Love and Saint Augustine* (Chicago: University of Chicago Press, 1998); and Reinhold Niebuhr, *Moral Man and Immoral Society: A Study in Ethics and Politics*, 2nd. ed. (Louisville: Westminster John Knox Press, 2013) and *The Nature and Destiny of Man: A Christian Interpretation*, 2 vols. (Louisville: Westminster John Knox Press, 1996).

3   Oliver O'Donovan, *Resurrection and Moral Order: An Outline for Evangelical Ethics*, 2nd edn (Grand Rapids, MI: William B. Eerdmans, 1994); Oliver O'Donovan, *The Desire of the Nations: Rediscovering the Roots of Political Theology*, 2nd edn (Cambridge: Cambridge University Press, 1999); Oliver O'Donovan, *The Ways of Judgment* (Grand Rapids, MI: William B. Eerdmans, 2005).

4   John Milbank, *Theology and Social Theory: Beyond Secular Reason* (Oxford: Blackwell, 1990).

5   Graham Ward, *Cities of God* (London: Routledge, 2000).

6   The first volume of this work has just been published as: Oliver O'Donovan, *Self, World, and Time: Ethics as Theology* (Grand Rapids, MI: William B. Eerdmans, 2013).

MODULE 11
IMPACT AND INFLUENCE TODAY

KEY POINTS

- *The City of God* still plays an important part in conversations on the relationship between religious and secular authorities in Western societies.

- *The City of God* is used to support an accommodating but self-limiting role for religion in contemporary politics.

- *The City of God* challenges absolutist positions in the debates over the proper relationship between Church and State.

Position

Today Augustine's *City of God* holds a privileged place in theological discussions, whether on the relationship between Church and State,[1] or over the constitution of human beings and their destiny in the age to come.[2] Outside the narrow confines of theology, the major conversation that *The City of God* directly informs is about the precise relationship between religious and secular authority in pluralist contexts. When society is multi-religious, what role should faiths take? Should the public sphere be devoid of all religious imagery and speech, or should it be bursting with religious color and vitality?

In the case of this debate, the terms have been structured around whether religious forms of authority are beneficial or harmful to the meaningful participation of those who do not identify with a dominant religious authority. For example, in a society that is majority Christian, do Muslims feel more or less comfortable speaking from a position of faith? And atheists?

> ❝ Secularized citizens, insofar as they act in their role as citizens, are not allowed to deny any truth potential to those who espouse religious worldviews, nor to deny their fellow believers the right to make contributions to public discussion in religious language. ❞
>
> Jürgen Habermas, *Dialectic of Secularism: On Reason and Religion*

This debate was re-energized in the 2000s in part because the influential German philosopher Jürgen Habermas* started to advocate for a more accommodating position toward religious expression. He used *The City of God* to remind Christians that they do not have an indisputable position from which to judge culture: the two cities are so inextricably intertwined that a purely "Christian" position would be impossible to espouse. Instead, Christians ought to advocate for the *common* good of the city, believing that the good of the "heavenly city" is provisionally found in and through a just and peaceful "earthly city." Anything beyond that is indiscernible from a human vantage point.

Interaction

Augustine's *City of God* plays a central role in debates over the relationship between religious belief and political commitment and action. While this represents a very narrow slice of *The City of God* itself, it gets to one of the central questions of the text: what do the "heavenly city" and the "earthly city" have to do with each other? Most scholars find answers in *The City of God* that directly challenge advocates on the extremes of the Church-State debate. On the one hand, *The City of God* reminds religious conservatives that the fate of the "heavenly city" is distinct from the rise or fall of any one worldly kingdom. On the other hand, it reminds those advocating a full separation of religion and politics that this position is unrealistic, because most people carry with them, in some shape or another, religious commitments such as belief in a supernatural power, transcendence, or the ultimate righting of wrongs. Are we to require religious voices to remain silent, while non-religious voices decide what is best for the community? *The City of God* is thus a reminder that a just political order is difficult to create and even harder to maintain. Any politics that tries to wish away those with whom the majority disagrees (or seems to disagree) is tantamount, for Augustine, to choosing to live isolated from all humanity, stranded on an island of one's own making.

The Continuing Debate

Many thinkers, institutions, and schools of thought are challenged by Augustine's accommodation of less-than-perfect politics. On one side are those who want to establish and enact laws that find their basis in religious commitment; on the other, those who want to rid political leadership of all Christian commitment. Both of these, the former represented by the "Religious Right"* in the United States, and the latter represented by "secularists," should find a challenge in Augustine's willingness to settle for imperfect peace in the "earthly city," as well as his admission of religious commitment to a share in public leadership. Because the Religious Right and secularist camps dominate the principal political groups in the United States, the Augustinian voice is usually drowned out in contemporary politics. There is thus no single coordinated response, and we should not expect one any time soon.

What, then, motivates the advocates of Augustinian compromise, in light of the overwhelming political and financial power of both the Religious Right and secularists? A mixture of intellectual, political, and economic motives. Intellectually speaking, many people, dissatisfied with such stark categories, want their religious beliefs to play some role in their lives, but do not think that that should shut out other ways of making decisions.[3] In other words, people reject a sharp division between private religious beliefs and public political commitments. Although neither do most people feel comfortable making full-throated appeals to their religious beliefs in support of a political program. There is for most people a messy middle ground between strict secularism and theocracy. *The City of God* has played a significant role in shaping how scholars and other interested parties attempt to figure out what place religion should have in the public sphere and how to ensure that it does not occlude the possibility of

NOTES

1   Robert Markus, *Saeculum: History and Society in the Theology of St Augustine* (Cambridge: Cambridge University Press, 1970).

2   Joseph Ratzinger, *Volk Und Haus Gottes in Augustins Lehre von Der Kirche* (Munich: Zink, 1954).

3   Nicholas Wolterstorff, *Understanding Liberal Democracy: Essays in Political Philosophy* (Oxford: Oxford University Press, 2012), 113–42.

WHERE NEXT?

KEY POINTS

- The future of Augustine's *City of God* lies in its academic readership.

- *The City of God* has great potential to contribute to debates about the changing status of religion in society today.

- Augustine's *City of God* is likely to continue to inform how religious practitioners renegotiate the relationship between faith and politics.

Potential

The influence of Augustine's *City of God* is likely to endure, but it is unclear in what form and among which institutions and people. In contemporary society, Augustine's ideas in *The City of God* are most often silently present as a philosophical background, rather than overtly called upon.[1] For example, "just war,"* a concept present in Augustine's work, has been an important subject of public debate in recent years, but Augustine is very rarely (if ever) directly appealed to.[2] His influence is omnipresent but unobserved.

In academia, Augustine's influence will be more explicit. Scholars of late antique and medieval literature will continue to read *The City of God* as a seminal text in the formation of the Western tradition. In so far as people will continue to inquire into the history of the Western intellectual tradition, Augustine's *City of God* will hold its value. If its endurance depends on its continued appropriation by contemporary philosophers and political theorists, its future is far from certain (despite its playing a central role in debates on the relationship between religion and politics).[3] The main challenge for philosophers and

> **❝** Through [Augustine's] doctrine of the two worlds,
> he sought salvation from all history, and insofar as
> he relativized earthly attempts at self-organization
> eschatologically, he taught that they should be
> interpreted all the more austerely. **❞**
>
> Reinhart Koselleck, *The Practice of Conceptual History: Timing History,
> Spacing Concepts*

political theorists is that Augustine's text is unashamedly theological in its approach to questions of historical development, justice, peace, and the relation between ecclesial* and secular institutions. For theologians, however, the fact that *The City of God* is a theological text is, of course, its strength. But theologians will have to conceive of new ways to employ Augustine's "great and difficult work" in secularized contexts.

Future Directions

In what ways, then, can *The City of God* inform a theologian today? This is a similar question to one that Augustine himself pursued in *The City of God*: how might the citizen of the "heavenly city" live in the "earthly city" while on pilgrimage? When does the pilgrim work for the peace and prosperity of the "earthly city," and when does he or she pursue projects more directly in line with specifically Christian ambitions? This set of questions drives to the heart of *The City of God*: can one genuinely be a dual citizen of both the earthly and heavenly cities? Although there has been—and will likely always be—much written on the two cities in the *City of God*, this theme will become more important as non-religious institutional contexts continue to proliferate.[4]

This is not to suggest that Christianity will disappear, but rather that the non-religious or not-explicitly-religious sphere will continue to grow. In Western cultures, particularly in Europe and North America, more people are identifying their religious beliefs outside the context of established religions.[5] Is *The City of God* relevant outside the institutional Church structure? Does it present a coherent vision of Christian existence without the institutional Church? These are the questions that theologians, and to some extent political theorists, will have to grapple with in the coming years. *The City of God*'s strength, when it comes to a changing religious landscape, is that at its core is the assumption that the society in which a Christian lives could at any moment turn hostile to his or her faith; its weakness is that it also assumes the institutional structure of the Church is the background of a "pilgrim life."

Summary

Augustine's *City of God* is a central text in the Western intellectual tradition. While it has often been read piecemeal or in excerpts, *The City of God* has continually proved to be a source of inspiration to scholars of theology, philosophy, history, and political theory. The great sweep of its narrative—from the beginning of Creation to the destruction of Rome in 410—and the theological sensitivity of its analysis of historical events will continue to make it a must-read for students of theology and politics.

Augustine himself is just as important as his text, if not more so. He was the author of scores of treatises, sermons, letters, and great works nearly equal to the size of *The City of God*. As a one-time imperial instructor of rhetoric at Milan and the Bishop of Hippo, Augustine was in a strong position to survey the damage and future reality of the Western Roman Empire after the Gothic invaders effectively wrested control of the territory from the Roman inhabitants. Today, Augustine is known as a "Father of the Church," a saint in both the Western and Eastern Christian traditions and a great intellect who preserved much of the philosophical thought of antiquity for the medieval age.

At root, Augustine's *City of God* is a text about Christian existence in a society that, while not openly hostile, is not completely at one with the way of life a Christian is called to live. In the wake of the destruction of Rome in 410, Augustine was forced to rethink the relationship between the historical destiny of Rome and the historical destiny of the Church. As cultures and nations continue to rise and fall, scholars must reconsider whether it is ever wise to identify the historical destiny of a faith tradition with a specific human institution. Augustine's text—more than any other text before or after—is aimed at helping us think about this question, which is no less pressing at the beginning of the twenty-first century than it was at the beginning of the fifth century.

NOTES

1   See, e.g., Charles Mathewes, *The Republic of Grace: Augustinian Thoughts for Dark Times* (Grand Rapids, MI: Eerdmans, 2010), 1-12.

2   Oliver O'Donovan, *The Just War Revisited* (Cambridge: Cambridge University Press, 2003).

3   Jonathan D. Teubner, *Prayer after Augustine: A Study in the Development of the Latin Tradition* (Oxford: Oxford University Press, 2018), 1-3.

4   See José Casanova, *Public Religions in the Modern World* (Chicago: University of Chicago Press, 1994), 11ff.

5   Pew Research Center, "The Future of World Religions: Population Growth Projections, 2010-2050," April 2, 2015: http://www.pewforum.org/2015/04/02/religious-projections-2010-2050/. Accessed on March 5, 2018.

GLOSSARY

GLOSSARY OF TERMS

Agnosticism: the view that the existence of God is unknown or unknowable.

Ancient Greece: cluster of Greek civilization dating from the ninth century BCE to c. 600 CE; these civilizations experienced one of the more intellectually creative periods in the history of the Mediterranean world.

Anglicanism: the Western Christian tradition that evolved out of the Church of England after it split from the Roman Catholic Church in the sixteenth century. It is the third largest Christian community, with 85 million members worldwide.

Anti-Pelagian Writings: anti-Pelagianism refers to Augustine's written response to the doctrines of Pelagius, a Christian theologian of the fourth–fifth century from what is now Britain. Pelagians believed that human moral effort was a vital part of salvation. Pelagius and Pelagianism were condemned at the Council of Carthage in 418. Augustine is widely identified as the originator of anti-Pelagianism.

Apocalypticism: the religious belief that the end of the world is imminent, often in one's own lifetime.

Apologetic Tradition: Christian theologians who wrote between the second and fourth centuries, including Tertullian, Cyprian, and Lactantius. Their works concentrated on defending Christianity from accusations and attempting to persuade others to convert.

Ascent of the Soul: a belief or doctrine that the human soul can undergo increasing purification and knowledge and ascend to be with God.

Bishop: an office in the Christian Church, charged with overseeing the beliefs and practices of Christians in a defined area called a diocese.

Blessedness: the state of being in full and complete happiness; often referred to as beatitude.

Christendom: refers to the period of European history where the church held formal or substantial informal powers over the political and economic affairs of states.

Christology: theological doctrines that relate to work and life of Jesus Christ

Church and State: refers to theories and policies regarding the relationship between Church (religion) and state (politics). It is often a shorthand for the separation of religion and politics as inscribed in the legal codes of the United States and France.

Church Fathers: a group of early authoritative Christian theologians, most from the fourth and fifth century.

Constantinople: capital city of the Eastern Roman Empire (330–1204 CE); present-day Istanbul, Turkey.

Corporate Spirituality: the non-individualistic focus of the spiritual life; often refers to the practice of praying, reading, and reflecting in groups.

Creation (doctrine): theological doctrines about and relating to God's bringing into existence of the world.

Dominican Order: a religious (monastic) order in the Roman Catholic Church, founded by the Spanish priest Dominic of Caleruega in France and approved by the Pope on December 22, 1216; often referred to as the "Order of Preachers."

Early Middle Ages: a transitional period between antiquity (ended c. 200 CE) and High Middle Ages (began c. 1200 CE); often referred to as the "Dark Ages."

Ecclesiology: theological doctrines relating to the Church.

Eusebianism: the belief that the Roman Empire was divinely elected to spread the Christian gospel in the world.

First Millennium of the Common Era: the first 1000 years after the traditional date of the Birth of Christ, i.e., year 0 AD.

Gothic Tribes/Invaders: East Germanic peoples who migrated to the Roman Empire in the fourth century; the Goths spoke their own language and followed a heretical branch of Christianity; the Gothic leader Alaric I led an army to sack Rome in 410.

Grace (doctrine): the grace of God is, for Augustine, an unmerited gift from God which enables the Christian's belief and sustains that belief through his or her life.

Justice: the ethical concept that regulates how you treat others; Augustine followed a Platonic definition of justice that stipulates that you give each person what they are due.

Just War: a doctrine of military ethics first propounded by Augustine. The doctrine classically stipulated the following: (1) a war must be waged by a properly instituted authority; (2) it must occur for a good and just purpose rather than for self-gain; and (3) peace must be a central motive of the violence.

Latin Christianity: refers to the Christian communities who spoke and wrote in Latin from the second to the sixteenth centuries in Europe and North Africa.

Latin West: refers to the portion of the Roman Empire that used Latin as its official language; often used to refer to those territories that were in the jurisdiction of Rome.

Liberal Arts: the subjects that were considered essential for a person to know in order to take part in civic affairs. Subjects included grammar, logic, rhetoric, arithmetic, geometry, music, and astronomy.

Monasticism: a religious way of life that renounces worldly pursuits in order to devote oneself fully to a life of prayer. First emerged in Christianity in the fourth century in Egypt and later developed in the Latin West under the influence of Augustine.

Pagan: a term for those who practice non-Christian religions, often used pejoratively in Christian writing.

Peace: the theological doctrine that describes perfect harmony between humans and God.

Pelagianism: a set of theological doctrines held by Pelagius and his followers that stipulated that human moral effort was a vital part of salvation. Pelagius and Pelagianism were condemned at the Council of Carthage in 418.

Pilgrimage (motif): a reoccurring theological theme that describes life in terms of a journey; often associated with walking long distances and physical hardship, such as a real pilgrim might experience while journeying to a pilgrimage site such as a saint's birthplace.

Platonism: Platonism is the philosophy or doctrine of the Greek philosopher Plato (428–348 BCE) or of his followers.

Political Theology: sub-field of theology that investigates how theological concepts relate to politics, society and economics.

Political Theory: the study of politics, liberty, justice, property, rights, law, and authority.

Protestant Reformation: the schism in Western Christianity initiated by John Wycliffe, John Hus, Martin Luther, John Calvin, and others. Among other things, the Reformers protested against corruption in the Vatican (the ruling body of the Roman Catholic Church).

Providence: divine foreknowledge of human events.

Radical Orthodoxy: a school of theologians founded by John Milbank; Radical Orthodoxy strongly critiques both conservative and liberal varieties of Christian politics, and advocates for distinctively Christian outlooks and policies.

Redemption (doctrine): Christian doctrine of salvation and deliverance from sin and its consequences.

Reformed Protestantism: the Christian communities that trace their origins to the Swiss Reformation via Scotland or the Netherlands.

Religious Right: a cluster of politically active groups that advocates socially conservative policies such as strict limits on abortion or a ban on gay marriage.

Renaissance: period in European history, roughly from the fourteenth to the seventeenth centuries, that experienced a growth in intellectual and creative industry. It is often seen as a bridge between the middle ages and modernity.

Rhetoric: the art of effective or persuasive speaking or writing.

Roman Catholic Church: the historic Christian community in the Latin West that looks to the Pope (Bishop of Rome) as the supreme earthly ruler of the Church.

Roman Empire: the period between 27 BCE and 478 CE, when an Emperor or set of Emperors decisively ruled the Roman territories that stretched from Britain to Africa and Spain to Turkey.

Roman North Africa: the territories of the Roman Empire in North Africa that were incorporated following the defeat of Carthage in the Third Punic War (146 BCE), roughly comprising present-day Tunisia, the northeast of modern-day Algeria, and the coast of Libya along the Gulf of Sirte. Carthage was considered the capital of the African province of Rome.

Sack of Rome (410): led by King Alaric, Gothic tribes raped and pillaged the city of Rome for three days beginning August 24, 410. This was a traumatic event in the history of the Roman Empire and the major impetus for Augustine's writing *The City of God*.

Salamanca School: a school of Renaissance Spanish and Portuguese theologians who were rooted in the intellectual work of Francisco de Vitoria; offered early economic and political theories they believed to be consonant with the Catholic tradition.

Science: derived from the Latin *scientia*, meaning "to know." Augustine used "science" to refer to knowledge that humans could know in this life.

Scripture: a set of writings, often referred to as the Bible, that are authoritative for Christianity and its devotees.

Secular: attitudes, activities, or beliefs that have no religious or spiritual basis.

Secularism: the political commitment to the separation of religious belief from public decision-making.

Teleology: explanation of events by the purposes they serve or their end result; this is opposed to explanations by causes.

Theocracy: a form of government in which God is the source from which all authority derives; often used to refer to regimes in which religious authorities directly rule.

Theological Anthropology: theological doctrines that concern human beings and their relationship with God; often addresses humans as created in the image of God, the effects of sin on humans' mind and body, and the restoration of human relationships with God.

Theological Virtues: the specifically Christian virtues which dispose one to conduct oneself in a morally good manner; traditionally "faith," "hope," and "love" are considered the three theological virtues.

Transnationalism: a social phenomenon and scholarly agenda that has developed from increased interconnectivity between people of different nations.

Trinity (doctrine): the Trinity is a Christian doctrine on the nature of God, which posits that God is Father, Son, and Holy Spirit, One God in three persons. Augustine dedicated one of his major works, *On The Trinity*, to this highly complex and controversial teaching.

Wisdom: in Augustine's usage, the variety of knowledge that God possesses and humans will possess in the next life.

PEOPLE MENTIONED IN THE TEXT

King Alaric I (370–410) was the king of the Visigoths 395–410. He is most famous for leading the Visigoths to sack Rome in 410.

Ambrose of Milan (337–397) was a theologian and bishop of Milan. Ambrose is most famous for his application of Platonism to understanding the Christian faith and for baptizing Augustine.

Thomas Aquinas (1225–74) was an Italian Dominican theologian and philosopher who is still widely read today. His magnum opus *Summa Theologiae* (*Summary of Theology*) is still standard reading for Catholic clergy.

Hannah Arendt (1906–75) was a Jewish philosopher who originally studied in Germany under Martin Heidegger and later taught at the University of Chicago. She is most famous for her responses to the Holocaust and Nazism.

Boethius (480–524/6) was a Roman senator, consul, and philosopher. Boethius is most famous for his *Consolation of Philosophy*, a meditation on free will that he wrote while awaiting his execution.

John Calvin (1509–64) was an influential theologian and pastor who played an important role in the Swiss Reformation, particularly in the politics of Geneva. His *Institutes of The Christian Religion* is a foundational text for Reformed Christianity.

John Cassian (360–435) was a celebrated monk and theologian who was a founding figure in Western monasticism. He is often associated with the Lerinian Monastery, a group of monks who sought to oppose the Augustinians' anti-Pelagianism.

Cicero (106–43 BCE) was a Roman philosopher, statesman, orator, and consul. Cicero was the main conduit of ancient Greek philosophical thought into the Latin-speaking cultures.

Cyprian of Carthage (210–258) was Bishop of Carthage in the tumultuous third century, when the Christian Church was violently persecuted. He was revered in North African Christianity in Augustine's day for his teachings on the authority of the church.

Robert Dodaro (b. 1955) is an American priest of the Catholic Church and until 2016 was the President of the Patristic Institute Augustinianum in Rome. Dodaro is known for his many specialist writings on the thought of Augustine.

Eusebius of Caesarea (263–339) was an historian of the early Church and theologian who supported Constantine I. Eusebius is best known for his belief that the Roman Empire was divinely elected to spread the Christian gospel.

Raymond Geuss (b. 1946) is Emeritus Professor of Philosophy at the University of Cambridge. Geuss is known for his many works in political philosophy that draw on nineteenth- and twentieth-century European philosophy.

Pope Gregory VII (1020–1085) was one of the Popes who sought to reform the church. Gregory VII is best known for the part he played in the Investiture Controversy, a dispute with the Holy Roman Emperor that affirmed the primacy of papal authority.

Jürgen Habermas (b. 1929) is a German philosopher and sociologist. Habermas is widely recognized as an authority on political and social philosophy, including the relation between religion and politics.

Jerome (347–420) was the most impressive Christian intellectual of his day – translator of the Bible from Hebrew and Greek into Latin, commentator on most books of Scripture and controversialist. He and Augustine corresponded on the interpretation of the biblical Epistle to the Galatians as well as on debates with Pelagius, a theologian from Britain who sought to give a prominent place to human effort in salvation.

Julian of Eclanum (386–455) was the Bishop of Eclanum (near Benevento, Italy) and leader of the Pelagian school and movement in the fifth century. Julian is mostly known for his spirited debates with Augustine on the origin of sin and the human soul.

Peter Iver Kaufman (b. 1946) is the George Matthews and Virginia Brinkley Modlin Chair in Leadership Studies at the University of Richmond. Kaufman is known for his studies in the political cultures of late antique, medieval, and early modern Europe.

Abraham Kuyper (1837–1920) was a Dutch reformed theologian and prime minister of the Netherlands 1901–1904. Kuyper is known as one of the leaders of "Neo-Calvinism," a school of theology that adapted John Calvin's political theology to nineteenth- and twentieth-century concerns.

Lactantius (240–320) is most famous as the advisor to the first Christian emperor, Constantine. He is also known for his political writings, which discuss the relation of the Christian religion to the Roman Empire.

Martin Luther (1483–1546) was initially an Augustinian friar, but subsequently disagreed with the Roman Catholic Church's teachings and initiated what we now know as the Reformation. The influence of Luther is hard to overstate: from his translation of the Bible into German, which became the basis for standardized German, to his doctrines on the sacraments of the Church, his works have profoundly influenced European civilization.

Alasdair MacIntyre (b. 1929) is a Scottish-American philosopher known for his contribution to moral and political philosophy. MacIntyre's *After Virtue* is widely recognized as one of the most important works of Anglophone moral and political philosophy in the twentieth century.

Flavius Marcellinus (4ᵗʰ–5ᵗʰ century) was a high official at the court of Roman Emperor Honorius. Marcellinus is known for his correspondence with Augustine.

Robert Markus (1925–2011) was a British medieval historian and theologian. Markus is best known for his scholarly work on Augustine, particularly his very influential book *Saeculum: History and Society in the Theology of St. Augustine.*

Charles Mathewes (b. 1969) is the Carolyn M. Barbour Professor of Religious Studies at the University of Virginia. Mathewes is known for his works on political theology and ethics, which draw on insights from Augustine's theology.

John Milbank (b. 1952) is a British theologian and social theorist who has been particularly critical of the "secularist" commitments of the contemporary Western nation state.

Reinhold Niebuhr (1892–1971) was an American theologian and political theorist. He has been made more popular today by references to his work from American President Barack Obama.

Oliver O'Donovan (b. 1945) is a British theologian and priest who taught at the Universities of Oxford and Edinburgh. O'Donovan is best known for his moral theology, which draws on the theology of Augustine.

Pelagius (4ᵗʰ–5ᵗʰ century) was a Christian theologian from what is now Britain. Pelagius is best known for his moral teachings, to which Augustine was strongly opposed.

Francesco Petrarch (1304–1374) was an Italian Renaissance scholar and poet. Petrarch is best known for his elegant and erudite poetry.

Plotinus (205–270) was a philosopher in the Platonic tradition. Historians credit Plotinus with founding the Neoplatonic school of philosophy.

Porphyry (234–305) was a student of Plotinus and a prominent philosopher in his own right. Although Porphyry wrote several of his own works of philosophy, he is most often remembered as a biographer of Plotinus and a compiler of that author's work.

John Rist (b. 1936) is a British scholar of ancient philosophy, classics and early Christian philosophy and theology. Rist is known for his contributions to the history of metaphysics and ethics.

Seneca (46 BCE–65 CE) was a Roman Stoic philosopher, statesman and one-time tutor to the Roman Emperor Nero. He is widely known for his moral epistles and other occasional works.

Tertullian (160–220) was a lawyer and Christian theologian. Tertullian was the first Christian author to produce a substantial corpus of theological writings in Latin.

Nicholas Trevet (1257–1334) was an English Dominican who studied at both Oxford and Paris. He is chiefly known for his theological and historical commentaries on classical texts, including Augustine's *City of God*.

Ernst Troeltsch (1865–1923) was a German theologian, historian and philosopher. Troeltsch was particularly influential in the field of Christian ethics and collaborated with Max Weber.

Varro (116–27 BCE) was a Roman scholar and writer. He was particularly influential on the educational curriculum of his day.

Thomas Waleys (13th–14th century) was a master of theology at Oxford University. He is known for a sermon on the beatific vision in 1333 and a commentary on *The City of God*.

Graham Ward (b. 1955) is the Regius Professor of Divinity at Oxford University. Ward is a priest in the Church of England and a prominent theologian in the Radical Orthodoxy school.

James Wetzel (b. 1959) holds the Augustinian Endowed Chair at the University of Villanova. Wetzel is known for his many writings on Augustine's philosophical and theological thought.

Rowan Williams (b. 1950) is the Baron of Oystermouth and a British theologian. Williams is best known for having been the Archbishop of Canterbury (Anglican) from 2002 to 2012.

WORKS CITED

WORKS CITED

Aquinas, Thomas. *Summa Theologiae*, n.d.

Arendt, Hannah. *The Human Condition*. 2nd edn. Chicago: University of Chicago Press, 1998.

Love and Saint Augustine. Chicago: University of Chicago Press, 1998.

Augustine. *The City of God Against the Pagans*. Edited by R. W. Dyson. Cambridge: Cambridge University Press, 1998.

Confessions. Translated by Henry Chadwick. Oxford: Oxford University Press, 1991.

Letters 1–99. Vol. 1. Translated by Roland Teske. Edited by John E. Rotelle. New York: New City Press, 2001.

Letters 100–155. Vol. 2. Translated by Roland Teske. Edited by Boniface Ramsey. New York: New City Press, 2003.

Letters 156–210. Vol. 3. Translated by Roland Teske. Edited by Boniface Ramsey. New York: New City Press, 2004.

Letters 211–270, 1*-29*. Vol. 4. Translated by Roland Teske. Edited by Boniface Ramsey. New York: New City Press, 2005.

Revisions. New York: New City Press, 2008.

Sermons 1–19. Vol. 1. Translated by Edmund Hill. Edited by John E. Rotelle. New York: New City Press, 1990.

Sermons 20–50. Vol. 2. Translated by Edmund Hill. Edited by John E. Rotelle. New York: New City Press, 1990.

Sermons 51–94. Vol. 3. Translated by Edmund Hill. Edited by John E. Rotelle. New York: New City Press, 1991.

Sermons 94A–147A. Vol. 4. Translated by Edmund Hill. Edited by John E. Rotelle. New York: New City Press, 1992.

Sermons 148–183. Vol. 5. Translated by Edmund Hill. Edited by John E. Rotelle. New York: New City Press, 1992.

Beutel, Albrecht. "Luther." In *Augustin Handbuch*, edited by Volker Henning Drecoll, 615–22. Tübingen: Mohr Siebeck, 2007.

Brown, Peter. *Through the Eye of a Needle: Wealth, the Fall of Rome, and the Making of Christianity in the West, 350–550AD*. Princeton, NJ: Princeton University Press, 2012.

Calvin, John. *Institutes of the Christian Religion*. Translated by Henry Beveridge. Peabody, MA: Hendrickson Publishers, 2007.

Casanova, José. *Public Religions in the Modern World*. Chicago: University of Chicago Press, 1994.

Dodaro, Robert. *Christ and the Just Society in the Thought of Augustine*. Cambridge: Cambridge University Press, 2004.

Elshtain, Jean Bethke. *Augustine and the Limits of Politics*. Notre Dame, IN: University of Notre Dame Press, 1995.

Fortin, Ernest L. "Augustine, the Arts, and Human Progress." In *Human Rights, Virtue, and the Common Good*, edited by J. Brian Benestad. London: Rowman and Littlefield, 1996.

Gorman, Michael M. *The Manuscript Traditions of the Works of St Augustine*. Firenze: Edizioni del Galluzzo, 2001.

"A Survey of the Oldest Manuscripts of St Augustine's De Ciuitate Dei." *Journal of Theological Studies* 33 (1982): 398–410.

Gregory, Eric. *Politics and the Order of Love: An Augustinian Ethic of Democratic Citizenship*. Chicago: University of Chicago Press, 2008.

Griffiths, Paul. "Secularity and the Saeculum." In *Augustine's City of God: A Critical Guide*, edited by James Wetzel. Cambridge: Cambridge University Press, 2012.

Hunter, James Davison. *To Change the World: The Irony, Tragedy, and Possibility of Christianity in the Late Modern World*. Oxford: Oxford University Press, 2010.

Kent, Bonnie. "Reinventing Augustine's Ethics: The Afterlife of City of God." In *Augustine's City of God: A Critical Guide*, edited by James Wetzel. Cambridge: Cambridge University Press, 2012.

Kuyper, Abraham. *Lectures on Calvinism*. Grand Rapids, MI: William B. Eerdmans, 1994.

Lancel, Serge. *Saint Augustine*. Translated by Antonia Nevill. London: SCM Press, 2002.

Markus, Robert. *Christianity and the Secular*. Notre Dame, IN: University of Notre Dame Press, 2006.

Saeculum: History and Society in the Theology of St Augustine. Cambridge: Cambridge University Press, 1970.

Mathewes, Charles. *The Republic of Grace: Augustinian Thoughts for Dark Times*. Grand Rapids, MI: Eerdmans Press, 2010.

Milbank, John. "'Postmodern Critical Augustinianism': A Short Summa in Response to Forty-Two Unasked Questions." *Modern Theology* 7, no. 3 (1991): 225–37.

Theology and Social Theory: Beyond Secular Reason. Oxford: Blackwell, 1990.

Niebuhr, Reinhold. *Beyond Tragedy: Essays on the Christian Interpretation of History*. New York: Charles Scribner's Sons, 1937.

Moral Man and Immoral Society: A Study in Ethics and Politics. Reprint. Louisville, KY: Westminster John Knox Press, 2002.

The Nature and Destiny of Man: A Christian Interpretation. Reprint. Louisville, KY: Westminster John Knox Press, 1996.

O'Daly, Gerard. *Augustine's City of God: A Reader's Guide*. Oxford: Clarendon Press, 1999.

O'Donnell, James J. "The Authority of Augustine." *Augustinian Studies* 22 (1991): 7–35.

O'Donovan, Oliver. *The Desire of the Nations: Rediscovering the Roots of Political Theology*. 2nd edn. Cambridge: Cambridge University Press, 1999.

Just War Revisited. Cambridge: Cambridge University Press, 2003.

"The Political Thought of City of God 19." In *Bonds of Imperfection: Christian Politics, Past and Present*, edited by Oliver O'Donovan and Joan Lockwood O'Donovan, 48–72. Grand Rapids, MI: William B. Eerdmans, 2004.

Resurrection and Moral Order: An Outline for Evangelical Ethics. 2nd edn. Grand Rapids, MI: William B. Eerdmans, 1994.

Self, World, and Time: Ethics as Theology. Grand Rapids, MI: William B. Eerdmans, 2013.

The Ways of Judgment. Grand Rapids, MI: William B. Eerdmans, 2005.

O'Meara, J. *Charter of Christendom: The Significance of the "City of God."* New York: Macmillan, 1961.

Pew Research Center, "The Future of World Religions: Population Growth Projectsions, 2010-2050" (April 2, 2015): http://www.pewforum. org/2015/04/02/religious-projections-2010-2050/.

Ratzinger, Joseph. *Volk Und Haus Gottes in Augustins Lehre von Der Kirche*. München: Zink, 1954.

Rist, John. *Augustine: Ancient Thought Baptized*. Cambridge: Cambridge University Press, 1994.

Saak, Eric. *Creating Augustine: Interpreting Augustine and Augustinianism in the Later Middle Ages*. Oxford: Oxford University Press, 2012.

Scanlon, Michael J. "The Augustinian Tradition: A Retrieval." *Augustinian Studies* 20 (1989): 61–92.

Stewart-Kroeker, Sarah. *Pilgrimage as Moral and Aesthetic Formation in Augustine's Thought*. Oxford: Oxford University Press, 2018.

Teubner, Jonathan D. *Prayer after Augustine: A Study in the Development of the Latin Tradition*. Oxford: Oxford University Press, 2018.

Troeltsch, Ernst. *Augustin, Die Christliche Antike Und Das Mittelalter. Im Anschluss an Die Schrift "De Civitate Dei."* Munich: R. Oldenbourg Verlag, 1915.

The Social Teachings of the Christian Churches. New York: Harper and Bros., 1960.

Van Nuffelen, Peter. *Orosius and the Rhetoric of History*. Oxford: Oxford University Press, 2012.

Van Oort, Johannes. "De Ciuitate Dei." In *Augustin Handbuch*, edited by Volker Henning Drecoll, translated by Emmanuel Rehfeld, 347–63. Tübingen: Mohr Siebeck, 2007.

Jerusalem and Babylon: A Study into Augustine's City of God and the Sources of His Doctrine of the Two Cities. Leiden: E.J. Brill, 1991.

Vessey, Mark. "The History of the Book: Augustine's City of God and post-Roman Cultural Memory." In *Augustine's City of God: A Critical Guide*, edited by James Wetzel, 14–32. Cambridge: Cambridge University Press, 2012.

Visser, Arnoud S. *Reading Augustine in the Reformation: The Flexibility of Intellectual Authority in Europe, 1500–1620*. Oxford: Oxford University Press, 2011.

Von Harnack, Adolf. *Lehrbuch Der Dogmengeschichte*. Vol. 3. Tübingen: Mohr Siebeck, 1910.

Ward, Graham. *Cities of God*. London: Routledge, 2000.

Wetzel, James. "Introduction." In *Augustine's City of God: A Critical Guide*, edited by James Wetzel, 1–13. Cambridge: Cambridge University Press, 2012.

Williams, Rowan. *On Augustine.* London: Bloomsbury: 2013.

Faith in the Public Square. London: Bloomsbury Continuum, 2012.

"Politics and the Soul: A Reading of the City of God." *Milltown Studies* 19/20 (1987): 55–72.

Wolterstorff, Nicholas. *Justice in Love*. Grand Rapids, MI: William B. Eerdmans, 2011.

Justice: Rights and Wrongs. Princeton, NJ: Princeton University Press, 2010.

Understanding Liberal Democracy: Essays in Political Philosophy. Oxford: Oxford University Press, 2012.

THE MACAT LIBRARY
BY DISCIPLINE

The Macat Library By Discipline

AFRICANA STUDIES

Chinua Achebe's *An Image of Africa: Racism in Conrad's Heart of Darkness*
W. E. B. Du Bois's *The Souls of Black Folk*
Zora Neale Huston's *Characteristics of Negro Expression*
Martin Luther King Jr's *Why We Can't Wait*
Toni Morrison's *Playing in the Dark: Whiteness in the American Literary Imagination*

ANTHROPOLOGY

Arjun Appadurai's *Modernity at Large: Cultural Dimensions of Globalisation*
Philippe Ariès's *Centuries of Childhood*
Franz Boas's *Race, Language and Culture*
Kim Chan & Renée Mauborgne's *Blue Ocean Strategy*
Jared Diamond's *Guns, Germs & Steel: the Fate of Human Societies*
Jared Diamond's *Collapse: How Societies Choose to Fail or Survive*
E. E. Evans-Pritchard's *Witchcraft, Oracles and Magic Among the Azande*
James Ferguson's *The Anti-Politics Machine*
Clifford Geertz's *The Interpretation of Cultures*
David Graeber's *Debt: the First 5000 Years*
Karen Ho's *Liquidated: An Ethnography of Wall Street*
Geert Hofstede's *Culture's Consequences: Comparing Values, Behaviors, Institutes and Organizations across Nations*
Claude Lévi-Strauss's *Structural Anthropology*
Jay Macleod's *Ain't No Makin' It: Aspirations and Attainment in a Low-Income Neighborhood*
Saba Mahmood's *The Politics of Piety: The Islamic Revival and the Feminist Subject*
Marcel Mauss's *The Gift*

BUSINESS

Jean Lave & Etienne Wenger's *Situated Learning*
Theodore Levitt's *Marketing Myopia*
Burton G. Malkiel's *A Random Walk Down Wall Street*
Douglas McGregor's *The Human Side of Enterprise*
Michael Porter's *Competitive Strategy: Creating and Sustaining Superior Performance*
John Kotter's *Leading Change*
C. K. Prahalad & Gary Hamel's *The Core Competence of the Corporation*

CRIMINOLOGY

Michelle Alexander's *The New Jim Crow: Mass Incarceration in the Age of Colorblindness*
Michael R. Gottfredson & Travis Hirschi's *A General Theory of Crime*
Richard Herrnstein & Charles A. Murray's *The Bell Curve: Intelligence and Class Structure in American Life*
Elizabeth Loftus's *Eyewitness Testimony*
Jay Macleod's *Ain't No Makin' It: Aspirations and Attainment in a Low-Income Neighborhood*
Philip Zimbardo's *The Lucifer Effect*

ECONOMICS

Janet Abu-Lughod's *Before European Hegemony*
Ha-Joon Chang's *Kicking Away the Ladder*
David Brion Davis's *The Problem of Slavery in the Age of Revolution*
Milton Friedman's *The Role of Monetary Policy*
Milton Friedman's *Capitalism and Freedom*
David Graeber's *Debt: the First 5000 Years*
Friedrich Hayek's *The Road to Serfdom*
Karen Ho's *Liquidated: An Ethnography of Wall Street*

John Maynard Keynes's *The General Theory of Employment, Interest and Money*
Charles P. Kindleberger's *Manias, Panics and Crashes*
Robert Lucas's *Why Doesn't Capital Flow from Rich to Poor Countries?*
Burton G. Malkiel's *A Random Walk Down Wall Street*
Thomas Robert Malthus's *An Essay on the Principle of Population*
Karl Marx's *Capital*
Thomas Piketty's *Capital in the Twenty-First Century*
Amartya Sen's *Development as Freedom*
Adam Smith's *The Wealth of Nations*
Nassim Nicholas Taleb's *The Black Swan: The Impact of the Highly Improbable*
Amos Tversky's & Daniel Kahneman's *Judgment under Uncertainty: Heuristics and Biases*
Mahbub Ul Haq's *Reflections on Human Development*
Max Weber's *The Protestant Ethic and the Spirit of Capitalism*

FEMINISM AND GENDER STUDIES

Judith Butler's *Gender Trouble*
Simone De Beauvoir's *The Second Sex*
Michel Foucault's *History of Sexuality*
Betty Friedan's *The Feminine Mystique*
Saba Mahmood's *The Politics of Piety: The Islamic Revival and the Feminist Subject*
Joan Wallach Scott's *Gender and the Politics of History*
Mary Wollstonecraft's *A Vindication of the Rights of Woman*
Virginia Woolf's *A Room of One's Own*

GEOGRAPHY

The Brundtland Report's *Our Common Future*
Rachel Carson's *Silent Spring*
Charles Darwin's *On the Origin of Species*
James Ferguson's *The Anti-Politics Machine*
Jane Jacobs's *The Death and Life of Great American Cities*
James Lovelock's *Gaia: A New Look at Life on Earth*
Amartya Sen's *Development as Freedom*
Mathis Wackernagel & William Rees's *Our Ecological Footprint*

HISTORY

Janet Abu-Lughod's *Before European Hegemony*
Benedict Anderson's *Imagined Communities*
Bernard Bailyn's *The Ideological Origins of the American Revolution*
Hanna Batatu's *The Old Social Classes And The Revolutionary Movements Of Iraq*
Christopher Browning's *Ordinary Men: Reserve Police Batallion 101 and the Final Solution in Poland*
Edmund Burke's *Reflections on the Revolution in France*
William Cronon's *Nature's Metropolis: Chicago And The Great West*
Alfred W. Crosby's *The Columbian Exchange*
Hamid Dabashi's *Iran: A People Interrupted*
David Brion Davis's *The Problem of Slavery in the Age of Revolution*
Nathalie Zemon Davis's *The Return of Martin Guerre*
Jared Diamond's *Guns, Germs & Steel: the Fate of Human Societies*
Frank Dikotter's *Mao's Great Famine*
John W Dower's *War Without Mercy: Race And Power In The Pacific War*
W. E. B. Du Bois's *The Souls of Black Folk*
Richard J. Evans's *In Defence of History*
Lucien Febvre's *The Problem of Unbelief in the 16th Century*
Sheila Fitzpatrick's *Everyday Stalinism*

The Macat Library By Discipline

LITERATURE

Chinua Achebe's *An Image of Africa: Racism in Conrad's Heart of Darkness*
Roland Barthes's *Mythologies*
Homi K. Bhabha's *The Location of Culture*
Judith Butler's *Gender Trouble*
Simone De Beauvoir's *The Second Sex*
Ferdinand De Saussure's *Course in General Linguistics*
T. S. Eliot's *The Sacred Wood: Essays on Poetry and Criticism*
Zora Neale Huston's *Characteristics of Negro Expression*
Toni Morrison's *Playing in the Dark: Whiteness in the American Literary Imagination*
Edward Said's *Orientalism*
Gayatri Chakravorty Spivak's *Can the Subaltern Speak?*
Mary Wollstonecraft's *A Vindication of the Rights of Women*
Virginia Woolf's *A Room of One's Own*

PHILOSOPHY

Elizabeth Anscombe's *Modern Moral Philosophy*
Hannah Arendt's *The Human Condition*
Aristotle's *Metaphysics*
Aristotle's *Nicomachean Ethics*
Edmund Gettier's *Is Justified True Belief Knowledge?*
Georg Wilhelm Friedrich Hegel's *Phenomenology of Spirit*
David Hume's *Dialogues Concerning Natural Religion*
David Hume's *The Enquiry for Human Understanding*
Immanuel Kant's *Religion within the Boundaries of Mere Reason*
Immanuel Kant's *Critique of Pure Reason*
Søren Kierkegaard's *The Sickness Unto Death*
Søren Kierkegaard's *Fear and Trembling*
C. S. Lewis's *The Abolition of Man*
Alasdair MacIntyre's *After Virtue*
Marcus Aurelius's *Meditations*
Friedrich Nietzsche's *On the Genealogy of Morality*
Friedrich Nietzsche's *Beyond Good and Evil*
Plato's *Republic*
Plato's *Symposium*
Jean-Jacques Rousseau's *The Social Contract*
Gilbert Ryle's *The Concept of Mind*
Baruch Spinoza's *Ethics*
Sun Tzu's *The Art of War*
Ludwig Wittgenstein's *Philosophical Investigations*

POLITICS

Benedict Anderson's *Imagined Communities*
Aristotle's *Politics*
Bernard Bailyn's *The Ideological Origins of the American Revolution*
Edmund Burke's *Reflections on the Revolution in France*
John C. Calhoun's *A Disquisition on Government*
Ha-Joon Chang's *Kicking Away the Ladder*
Hamid Dabashi's *Iran: A People Interrupted*
Hamid Dabashi's *Theology of Discontent: The Ideological Foundation of the Islamic Revolution in Iran*
Robert Dahl's *Democracy and its Critics*
Robert Dahl's *Who Governs?*
David Brion Davis's *The Problem of Slavery in the Age of Revolution*

The Macat Library By Discipline

Alexis De Tocqueville's *Democracy in America*
James Ferguson's *The Anti-Politics Machine*
Frank Dikotter's *Mao's Great Famine*
Sheila Fitzpatrick's *Everyday Stalinism*
Eric Foner's *Reconstruction: America's Unfinished Revolution, 1863-1877*
Milton Friedman's *Capitalism and Freedom*
Francis Fukuyama's *The End of History and the Last Man*
John Lewis Gaddis's *We Now Know: Rethinking Cold War History*
Ernest Gellner's *Nations and Nationalism*
David Graeber's *Debt: the First 5000 Years*
Antonio Gramsci's *The Prison Notebooks*
Alexander Hamilton, John Jay & James Madison's *The Federalist Papers*
Friedrich Hayek's *The Road to Serfdom*
Christopher Hill's *The World Turned Upside Down*
Thomas Hobbes's *Leviathan*
John A. Hobson's *Imperialism: A Study*
Samuel P. Huntington's *The Clash of Civilizations and the Remaking of World Order*
Tony Judt's *Postwar: A History of Europe Since 1945*
David C. Kang's *China Rising: Peace, Power and Order in East Asia*
Paul Kennedy's *The Rise and Fall of Great Powers*
Robert Keohane's *After Hegemony*
Martin Luther King Jr.'s *Why We Can't Wait*
Henry Kissinger's *World Order: Reflections on the Character of Nations and the Course of History*
John Locke's *Two Treatises of Government*
Niccolò Machiavelli's *The Prince*
Thomas Robert Malthus's *An Essay on the Principle of Population*
Mahmood Mamdani's *Citizen and Subject: Contemporary Africa And The Legacy Of Late Colonialism*
Karl Marx's *Capital*
John Stuart Mill's *On Liberty*
John Stuart Mill's *Utilitarianism*
Hans Morgenthau's *Politics Among Nations*
Thomas Paine's *Common Sense*
Thomas Paine's *Rights of Man*
Thomas Piketty's *Capital in the Twenty-First Century*
Robert D. Putman's *Bowling Alone*
John Rawls's *Theory of Justice*
Jean-Jacques Rousseau's *The Social Contract*
Theda Skocpol's *States and Social Revolutions*
Adam Smith's *The Wealth of Nations*
Sun Tzu's *The Art of War*
Henry David Thoreau's *Civil Disobedience*
Thucydides's *The History of the Peloponnesian War*
Kenneth Waltz's *Theory of International Politics*
Max Weber's *Politics as a Vocation*
Odd Arne Westad's *The Global Cold War: Third World Interventions And The Making Of Our Times*

POSTCOLONIAL STUDIES

Roland Barthes's *Mythologies*
Frantz Fanon's *Black Skin, White Masks*
Homi K. Bhabha's *The Location of Culture*
Gustavo Gutiérrez's *A Theology of Liberation*
Edward Said's *Orientalism*
Gayatri Chakravorty Spivak's *Can the Subaltern Speak?*

PSYCHOLOGY

Gordon Allport's *The Nature of Prejudice*
Alan Baddeley & Graham Hitch's *Aggression: A Social Learning Analysis*
Albert Bandura's *Aggression: A Social Learning Analysis*
Leon Festinger's *A Theory of Cognitive Dissonance*
Sigmund Freud's *The Interpretation of Dreams*
Betty Friedan's *The Feminine Mystique*
Michael R. Gottfredson & Travis Hirschi's *A General Theory of Crime*
Eric Hoffer's *The True Believer: Thoughts on the Nature of Mass Movements*
William James's *Principles of Psychology*
Elizabeth Loftus's *Eyewitness Testimony*
A. H. Maslow's *A Theory of Human Motivation*
Stanley Milgram's *Obedience to Authority*
Steven Pinker's *The Better Angels of Our Nature*
Oliver Sacks's *The Man Who Mistook His Wife For a Hat*
Richard Thaler & Cass Sunstein's *Nudge: Improving Decisions About Health, Wealth and Happiness*
Amos Tversky's *Judgment under Uncertainty: Heuristics and Biases*
Philip Zimbardo's *The Lucifer Effect*

SCIENCE

Rachel Carson's *Silent Spring*
William Cronon's *Nature's Metropolis: Chicago And The Great West*
Alfred W. Crosby's *The Columbian Exchange*
Charles Darwin's *On the Origin of Species*
Richard Dawkin's *The Selfish Gene*
Thomas Kuhn's *The Structure of Scientific Revolutions*
Geoffrey Parker's *Global Crisis: War, Climate Change and Catastrophe in the Seventeenth Century*
Mathis Wackernagel & William Rees's *Our Ecological Footprint*

SOCIOLOGY

Michelle Alexander's *The New Jim Crow: Mass Incarceration in the Age of Colorblindness*
Gordon Allport's *The Nature of Prejudice*
Albert Bandura's *Aggression: A Social Learning Analysis*
Hanna Batatu's *The Old Social Classes And The Revolutionary Movements Of Iraq*
Ha-Joon Chang's *Kicking Away the Ladder*
W. E. B. Du Bois's *The Souls of Black Folk*
Émile Durkheim's *On Suicide*
Frantz Fanon's *Black Skin, White Masks*
Frantz Fanon's *The Wretched of the Earth*
Eric Foner's *Reconstruction: America's Unfinished Revolution, 1863-1877*
Eugene Genovese's *Roll, Jordan, Roll: The World the Slaves Made*
Jack Goldstone's *Revolution and Rebellion in the Early Modern World*
Antonio Gramsci's *The Prison Notebooks*
Richard Herrnstein & Charles A Murray's *The Bell Curve: Intelligence and Class Structure in American Life*
Eric Hoffer's *The True Believer: Thoughts on the Nature of Mass Movements*
Jane Jacobs's *The Death and Life of Great American Cities*
Robert Lucas's *Why Doesn't Capital Flow from Rich to Poor Countries?*
Jay Macleod's *Ain't No Makin' It: Aspirations and Attainment in a Low Income Neighborhood*
Elaine May's *Homeward Bound: American Families in the Cold War Era*
Douglas McGregor's *The Human Side of Enterprise*
C. Wright Mills's *The Sociological Imagination*

The Macat Library By Discipline

Thomas Piketty's *Capital in the Twenty-First Century*
Robert D. Putman's *Bowling Alone*
David Riesman's *The Lonely Crowd: A Study of the Changing American Character*
Edward Said's *Orientalism*
Joan Wallach Scott's *Gender and the Politics of History*
Theda Skocpol's *States and Social Revolutions*
Max Weber's *The Protestant Ethic and the Spirit of Capitalism*

THEOLOGY

Augustine's *Confessions*
Benedict's *Rule of St Benedict*
Gustavo Gutiérrez's *A Theology of Liberation*
Carole Hillenbrand's *The Crusades: Islamic Perspectives*
David Hume's *Dialogues Concerning Natural Religion*
Immanuel Kant's *Religion within the Boundaries of Mere Reason*
Ernst Kantorowicz's *The King's Two Bodies: A Study in Medieval Political Theology*
Søren Kierkegaard's *The Sickness Unto Death*
C. S. Lewis's *The Abolition of Man*
Saba Mahmood's *The Politics of Piety: The Islamic Revival and the Feminist Subject*
Baruch Spinoza's *Ethics*
Keith Thomas's *Religion and the Decline of Magic*

Macat Disciplines

Access the greatest ideas and thinkers across entire disciplines, including

CRIMINOLOGY

Michelle Alexander's
The New Jim Crow: Mass Incarceration in the Age of Colorblindness

Michael R. Gottfredson & Travis Hirschi's
A General Theory of Crime

Elizabeth Loftus's
Eyewitness Testimony

Richard Herrnstein & Charles A. Murray's
The Bell Curve: Intelligence and Class Structure in American Life

Jay Macleod's
Ain't No Makin' It: Aspirations and Attainment in a Low-Income Neighborhood

Philip Zimbardo's
The Lucifer Effect

Macat analyses are available from all good bookshops and libraries.

Access hundreds of analyses through one, multimedia tool.

Macat Disciplines

Access the greatest ideas and thinkers across entire disciplines, including

Postcolonial Studies

Roland Barthes's *Mythologies*
Frantz Fanon's *Black Skin, White Masks*
Homi K. Bhabha's *The Location of Culture*
Gustavo Gutiérrez's *A Theology of Liberation*
Edward Said's *Orientalism*
Gayatri Chakravorty Spivak's *Can the Subaltern Speak?*

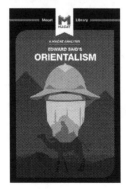

Macat analyses are available from all good bookshops and libraries.

Access hundreds of analyses through one, multimedia tool.

Join free for one month **library.macat.cc**

Printed in the United States
by Baker & Taylor Publisher Services